Queer and Feminist Theories of Narrative

This book argues for the importance of narrative theories which consider gender and sexuality through the analysis of a diverse range of texts and media.

Classical Narratology, an allegedly neutral descriptive system for features of narrative, has been replaced by a diverse set of theories which are attentive to the contexts in which narratives are composed and received. Issues of gender and sexuality have, nevertheless, been sidelined by new strands which consider, for example, cognitive, transmedial, national or historical inflections instead. Through consideration of texts including the MTV series *Faking It* and the papers of a nineteenth-century activist, *Queer and Feminist Theories of Narrative* heeds the original call of feminist narratologists for the consideration of a broader and larger corpus of material. Through analysis of issues including the popular representation of lesbian desire, the queer narrative voice, invisibility and power in the digital age, embodiment and cognitive narratology, reading and racial codes, this book argues that a named strand of narrative theory which employs feminist and queer theories as intersectional vectors is contemporary and urgent.

The chapters in this book were originally published as a special issue of the journal *Textual Practice*.

Tory Young teaches Contemporary and Modernist Literature at ARU, Cambridge, UK. She is currently writing a monograph about 21st-Century Love Stories, which reconsiders plot and desire in popular and literary fiction. She is the author of a practical guide for students *Studying English Literature* (CUP).

Queer and Feminist Theories of Narrative

Edited by
Tory Young

LONDON AND NEW YORK

First published 2021
by Routledge
2 Park Square, Milton Park, Abingdon, Oxon, OX14 4RN

and by Routledge
52 Vanderbilt Avenue, New York, NY 10017

Routledge is an imprint of the Taylor & Francis Group, an informa business

© 2021 Taylor & Francis

All rights reserved. No part of this book may be reprinted or reproduced or utilised in any form or by any electronic, mechanical, or other means, now known or hereafter invented, including photocopying and recording, or in any information storage or retrieval system, without permission in writing from the publishers.

Trademark notice: Product or corporate names may be trademarks or registered trademarks, and are used only for identification and explanation without intent to infringe.

British Library Cataloguing-in-Publication Data
A catalogue record for this book is available from the British Library

ISBN13: 978-0-367-68109-8

Typeset in Minion Pro
by codeMantra

Publisher's Note
The publisher accepts responsibility for any inconsistencies that may have arisen during the conversion of this book from journal articles to book chapters, namely the inclusion of journal terminology.

Disclaimer
Every effort has been made to contact copyright holders for their permission to reprint material in this book. The publishers would be grateful to hear from any copyright holder who is not here acknowledged and will undertake to rectify any errors or omissions in future editions of this book.

Contents

	Citation Information	vi
	Notes on Contributors	viii
	Introduction: Futures for feminist and queer narratology *Tory Young*	1
1	Queering narrative voice *Susan S. Lanser*	10
2	Rethinking the subject in feminist research: narrative personae and stories of 'the real' *Maria Tamboukou*	25
3	'We fuck and friends don't fuck': BFFs, lesbian desire, and queer narratives *Sam McBean*	42
4	A moving target – cognitive narratology and feminism *Karin Kukkonen*	58
5	Invisibility and power in the digital age: issues for feminist and queer narratology *Tory Young*	75
6	The unspeakable, the unnarratable, and the repudiation of epiphany in 'Recitatif': a collaboration between linguistic and literary feminist narratologies *Robyn Warhol and Amy Shuman*	91
	Index	111

Citation Information

The chapters in this book were originally published in *Textual Practice*, volume 32, issue 6 (2018). When citing this material, please use the original page numbering for each article, as follows:

Introduction
Futures for feminist and queer narratology
Tory Young
Textual Practice, volume 32, issue 6 (2018) pp. 913–921

Chapter 1
Queering narrative voice
Susan S. Lanser
Textual Practice, volume 32, issue 6 (2018) pp. 923–937

Chapter 2
Rethinking the subject in feminist research: narrative personae and stories of 'the real'
Maria Tamboukou
Textual Practice, volume 32, issue 6 (2018) pp. 939–955

Chapter 3
'We fuck and friends don't fuck': BFFs, lesbian desire, and queer narratives
Sam McBean
Textual Practice, volume 32, issue 6 (2018) pp. 957–972

Chapter 4
A moving target – cognitive narratology and feminism
Karin Kukkonen
Textual Practice, volume 32, issue 6 (2018) pp. 973–989

Chapter 5
Invisibility and power in the digital age: issues for feminist and queer narratology
Tory Young
Textual Practice, volume 32, issue 6 (2018) pp. 991–1006

Chapter 6
The unspeakable, the unnarratable, and the repudiation of epiphany in 'Recitatif':
a collaboration between linguistic and literary feminist narratologies
Robyn Warhol and Amy Shuman
Textual Practice, volume 32, issue 6 (2018) pp. 1007–1025

For any permission-related enquiries please visit:
http://www.tandfonline.com/page/help/permissions

Contributors

Karin Kukkonen Department of Literature, Area Studies and European Languages, University of Oslo, Oslo, Norway.

Susan S. Lanser Comparative Literature, English, and Women's, Gender, and Sexuality Studies, Brandeis University, Waltham, MA, USA.

Sam McBean Department of English, Queen Mary University of London, London, UK.

Amy Shuman Department of English, Ohio State University, Columbus, OH, USA.

Maria Tamboukou Department of Social Sciences, University of East London, London, UK.

Robyn Warhol Department of English, Ohio State University, Columbus, OH, USA.

Tory Young English & Media, Anglia Ruskin University, Cambridge, UK.

INTRODUCTION
Futures for feminist and queer narratology
Tory Young

In a survey of concepts and theories of narrative in 2000, Brian Richardson noted that '[t]he history of modern narrative theory is more accurately depicted as a cluster of contiguous histories rather than a single, comprehensive narrative'. He also reported that 'Feminism ... has (as should be expected) utterly and fruitfully transformed narrative theory and analysis.'[1] Taken together, these claims suggest that feminist narratology, as it was formulated by Susan S. Lanser in 1986, had not developed as a distinct poetics, but rather that the influence of feminist principles and methodologies had been felt more widely across different strands of narrative theory and textual analysis.[2] What is the evidence for this? Many of the new directions in modern theories of narrative, and in post-classical narratology in particular, are more attentive to context than their formalist predecessors, and some of these contextual interests emerge from feminist frameworks or issues in gender studies. There are very few monographs that openly identify with something called *feminist narratology* – Ruth Page's *Literary and Linguistic Approaches to Feminist Narratology*[3] is one – and many more feminist works that attend to the relationship between narrative structure and sexuality more generally, as Lanser herself acknowledged in her original essay, in the manner of Judith Roof's *Come As You Are*.[4] Is it then the case that feminist and gender-based narratological readings of texts have not so much been absorbed by different strands of narrative theory, but rather that narratological methods and issues have found their way into a broader tradition of feminist and intersectional reading? If so, does feminist narratology have a distinct identity at all, beyond being a contribution to, perhaps a slight sharpening of feminism's analytical tools?

It can certainly appear, in the twenty-first century, that feminist narratology is still not regarded as a separate or distinct project in narratology as such. In 2011, Greta Olson's *Current Trends in Narratology* makes no mention of feminism, gender or sexuality, instead describing three broad strands: cognitive, transmedial and nationally or historically inflected narratologies.[5] It would make no sense to suppose that feminism had not been a significant force in at least the last two of these categories, and much more sense to agree with Richardson that its influence and relevance is more diffuse. The call in transmedial narratology, for example, to apply existing typologies to new objects of study echoes one of Lanser's demands from the start that narratology should build its findings on a much broader and more diverse corpus of texts, which must expand as new narrative medias develop. At the same time, the idea that gender-based narratology has been so successful that it has achieved a kind of invisibility is a cause for concern, and a tenet that is both pursued and questioned by the contributors to this special edition of *Textual Practice*.

Early objections to the idea of feminist narratology, as a kind of contamination of the neutral descriptive system of classical narratology by ideologically motivated analysis, have long been discounted. Nilli Diengott's angry response to Lanser's 1986 manifesto, for example, that feminism had no business with narratology, has been overruled by what has happened since 1988, and as Richardson described the situation in 2000; to her question of whether feminist critics can desist in the 'attempt to appropriate to their feminist enterprise others of a totally different nature?', we might want to answer that the difference has since been eroded or erased.[6] That is to say, the slightly confusing language that has emerged in contemporary narrative theory, that named formalism and structuralism as the classical phase of narratology, also announced a broad post-classical epoch in which the founding assumptions of semiology were developed, challenged and rejected, and in this transition the precepts most obviously hostile to ideological critique or contextual study were systematically displaced. It no longer seems possible to regard narratology as a neutral linguistic science, nor to close the gates to the diaspora of approaches which considered the contexts of sexual difference, desire and psychoanalysis, race, history, and more recently queer theory, and cognitive or mind-based theories. Gerald Prince's resistance to Lanser's call for political contexts, his call for narratologists to resist 'the interpretative temptation' (which belongs to criticism not narratology), may be upheld in some determined branches, but all around them, others flourish in the new post-classical mix.[7] Theories of narrative, like forms of narrative themselves, are permanently in flux, and accordingly, the formulation of feminist narratology by its named practitioners has dissembled into diverse queer and feminist theories of narrative. The development of feminist narratology is doing nothing other than shadowing the complicated and unplottable development of feminism at large, which was always factional, formed into a complex kind of academic unity in gender studies, forged new relationships and alliances with emerging areas such as queer theory and stands now as one vector in intersectional approaches. Many of the basic analytical problems of so-called classical narratology – the relationships between story and plot, narrator and author, and the text and its analysis – are still present in this expanded narratological universe, but they tend to be addressed in very specific contexts and often at the expense of the global systems and master sciences that presided over narrative semiology in its classical phase.

Many of the trajectories of feminist literary theory and criticism are discernible in the history of feminist narratology, whether because feminism absorbed narratological methods or because narratology incorporated feminist perspectives. Some of the early calls for a narratology inflected or influenced by feminism were for a larger corpus of texts: a diversification in the object of study that would challenge, modify or deny 'a universalizing model of narrative'.[8] Sometimes the need for rudimentary feminist arguments for an increased attention to texts by women was compelling; Robyn Warhol found that only 2 of Prince's 80-plus examples in his 'Introduction to the Study of the Narratee' were drawn from female-authored texts. Sometimes these interventions would bring to light those elements of narrative which would be affected by a consideration of gender and which would not.[9] Lanser thought that whilst 'theories of plot and story may need to change substantially [...] theories of time' might not, a line of thought which has been interestingly reshaped by subsequent queer theorists including Lee Edelman, as Sam McBean points out in her essay in this volume, and which is also addressed by Maria Tamboukou's 'conceptualisation of narrative as force'.[10] Using a letter from a nineteenth-century anthology which seems to utilise an unusual double construction to send a private message in a public missive, Lanser sought to demonstrate the importance of the rhetorical context of narrative in a way that broke new narratological ground. The rhetorical complexities of the letter presented, for Lanser, a range of analytical problems around its authenticity, its censorship and its status as a parody of the form, and enabled Lanser to open a new set of questions – about 'narrative level, context and voice' – for 'the plot that may be generated by the relationship between the narrator and narratee'.[11] These early developments, in other words, combined some of the old problematics of narrative structure and address with some new questions about the gender of voice to produce a different kind of encounter between narrative voice and its context, and a different kind of deployment of narratological tools. One of the problems in Lanser's developing approach in *The Narrative Act* and *Fictions of Authority* was her identification of a narrator with a gendered human.[12] In 2011, Robyn Warhol and Lanser held a symposium on queer and feminist interventions and in the collection that followed Lanser recasts this earlier problematic as she outlines her development from a feminist narratology to a queer one:

> my own work on narrative voice has argued that the gender of an otherwise unmarked heterodiegetic (i.e. 'third person') narrator will derive from the gender of the textually inscribed author. So compelled was I to attribute gender to narrators that in some quarters that linkage came to be dubbed as 'Lanser's rule.' I speculated, however, that the authority given to male voices might override that link in the case of a woman writer, in effect already queering my own proposition.[13]

In the works that have self-identified as feminist narratology, Free Indirect Discourse (in which the voice of a character and the narrator are merged and the answers to the questions 'who speaks?' and 'who sees?' may be different) has been a central concept for this kind of argument that the novel has always specialised in unidentifiable identities and undecidable voices, from long before such things were known, and perhaps in ways that were simply unknown, in the theory of gender and sexuality. Patricia Matson's essay on Virginia Woolf's textual politics, in Kathy Mezei's collection *Ambiguous Discourse*, reads *Mrs Dalloway* in this light 'as a novel that involves readers in a heterogeneous, exploratory, and spiralling process', one which refuses the reader mastery by collapsing the binaries upon which conventional realism depends, dispersing focalisation, and frequently employing the word 'it' in long sentences which defer 'its' meaning.[14] Here, the imprecision or ambiguity of the pronoun allows the unspeakable to be spoken of. In this kind of approach to the imprecision of pronouns, we can see an articulation of problems also at work in contemporary thinking about a more widespread kind of pronoun use: the deliberate deployment (sometimes considered as grammatically 'inaccurate') of the pronouns 'they' and 'them' to refer to a single subject. In such cases, gender is not specified as part of a refusal of a binary-gendered identity, as if non-binary-gendered identities were linguistically known before they were accepted, a queer disruption to linear time examined by both McBean and Young in their essays in this edition.

Is the problem of depicting gender fluidity, now attracting much media attention, already solved through the use of plural pronouns? It has been there all along but only now that we see it more widely in the world can we recognise it? Lanser is understandably cautious but suggests 'putting to the narratological test D.A. Miller's proposal that formal innovation may be the displaced project of queer fiction'.[15] Lanser asks:

> Is it accidental, for example that Henry James, Virginia Woolf, Dorothy Richardson, Marcel Proust, Colette, Nella Larsen, Djuna Barnes, Katharine Mansfield, and Gertrude Stein – and maybe James Joyce – were queer(ish) folk as well as modernists who pioneered the practice of FID?

By asking this question, Lanser proposes a connection, perhaps an implicit affiliation, between an author's sexuality and narrative form, following a kind of inductive method through which queerness is uncovered in texts rather than discovered deductively through a universal systemic framework.[16]

In 'Queering Narrative Voice', Lanser returns to the question of narrative voice and the body, taking 'up all three meanings of the verb "to queer" – to transgress normative sexualities, to dismantle sexual fixities, and to dismantle all fixities – to ask what we might gain by bringing any one of these to bear on fictional narrators'. Her series of essays in gender and sexuality studies has always hoped for the emergence of first a feminist narratology, then a queer one but she finds in 2017 that the latter 'remains underdeveloped' and here argues against the fears of others, that a feminist and queer approach can be combined without loss to the ideological aims of either. At once recognising the benefits of a fluid intermingling of these meanings of 'queer' for her status as a 'queer-invested scholar', here Lanser writes as a narratologist to see precisely how each is 'constrained [...] by its narrative environment'. In seeking 'to critique the pervasive practice of tautological reading, whereby queer author = queer narrator and to emphasize instead the value of asking how a queer narrative voice might be coded through formal practices', Lanser acknowledges that she has to rethink the 'assumption that has been deeply rooted in [her] formulations of a feminist narratology: that the gender of an author carries into the gender of an unmarked narrative voice'. This reconsideration is taken up not only in her essay but those of Tamboukou and Kukkonen in this edition too.

It does not follow that the experimental text is forged by the queer body, nor that realism is a form which promotes heteronormativity, but rather that narratological perspectives might have some purchase on the relation between surface narrative features on one hand and the gendered body, particularly when supplemented by contextual or rhetorical frames. Back in 1988, Nicole Brossard stated that a 'lesbian who does not reinvent the word is a lesbian in the process of disappearing', but in this edition, we interrogate the alignment of authorial body with text.[17] McBean challenges it through examination of the most banal of forms, an MTV sitcom. She shows how the Best Friends Forever (BFF) epithet, which seems to conceal same-sex relationships under a veneer of friendship, may actually enable queer narratives. McBean looks at MTV's *Faking It* (2014–2016), a sitcom in which two female high-school students, Amy and Karma, are misrecognised as lesbians, a reversal of the social-media trend in which celebrity women's accounts were scoured for signs of friendship, which in fact masked sexual and romantic relationships. McBean connects 'this contemporary erasure [...] to a longer history that explores the textual invisibility of the lesbian'. At the alternative school Amy and Karma attend, lesbian identity is a way of attaining status, so the two embrace rather than deny it, and the faking of their relationship leads to strong feelings of desire in Amy for Karma. McBean's essay demonstrates that *Faking It* 'in binding the lesbian story to a narrative of friendship, [...] challenges a contemporary politics that refuses or resists friendship as only a "cover" for lesbianism'. McBean reconsiders the relationship between a coherent sexual or gender identity, power and visibility (as do Warhol and Shuman, and Young in this issue). Her essay does so with recourse to the 'substantial body of queer work that considers queerness a product of a relationship to temporality', but crucially, brings the theory to the analysis of popular media. McBean shows that '*Faking It* offers a queerer chronology'; instead of being 'born gay' 'Amy's desire is awakened precisely because she fakes being a lesbian for her BFF'. Linear chronology is disrupted, she argues, so that the conventional 'coming out' scene also involves a queering of the serial form where Amy and Karma worry 'about how long the eventfulness of their relationship can be sustained'.

Warhol and Lanser are committed to 'pluralist *bricolage*' like 'Franco Moretti's maps, graphs, and trees' or 'Gilles Deleuze and Félix Guattari's concept of assemblages'.[18] Their call, which shares the preference for plurality over the universal in the original call, turns to the body, not of the author, but of the reader;

> And, too, after thirty years of dwelling on the politics of form, feminist and queer narrative theories may be ready to turn from poetics and hermeneutics to take on a politicized aesthetics, conceived perhaps as an erotics of narrative that would be focused on the reader's body.[19]

The focus on the reader's body has an unexpected connection to another major strand in narrative research, however antithetical it might appear to a political queer or feminist narratology, namely the tendency outlined by Olsen towards a cognitive narratology. In a way that significantly departs from the orientations of classical narratologists, mind-based theories are contextual, transmedial and concerned with the processes and cues which inform interpretations. As Karin Kukkonen points out 'Cognitive narratology does not traditionally consider gender perspectives [...] because the gendering of brains into "male" and "female" is deeply problematic'; so problematic in fact that *The Living Handbook of Narratology* claims even those 'working on issues that fall within this domain do not necessarily identify their work as cognitive-narratological, and might even resist association with the approach'.[20] In moving from the brain 'to the larger connections between the brain, body and their situatedness in the world', Kukkonen proposes new directions for feminist narratology that are actually enabled by the cognitive turn, and explores these possibilities through a compelling reading of Hilary Mantel's short story 'The Assassination of Margaret Thatcher'. Kukkonen acknowledges that the contexts within which Mantel may be usually studied (as a 'modern, British, female' writer) are those which, for a cognitive narratologist, 'tend to be side-lined in favour of seemingly neutral notions such as narrators, focalisers (or fictional minds), prototypical story scripts, as well as fictional worlds'. The bind of a feminist cognitive narratology, she argues, is that the recognition of gender at the cognitive level – if male and female brains are proposed as different – invites a charge of 'neurosexism', but if there is no difference then gender is not a pertinent aspect of enquiry. Kukkonen's proposition employs 'current perspectives on cognition as an embodied process of probability and prediction that connect easily to cultural modes of meaning-making' and enters them 'into a conversation with feminist narratology and feminist literary theory'. In Mantel's story, an assassin targeting Thatcher invades the flat of a curiously dispassionate narrator; the two figures (narrator and assassin) are not explicitly identified as a middle-class female and a working-class male but are figured as such through their language use alone. For Kukkonen, '[g]ender-oriented sociolinguistics [...] and the embodied approach in cognitive linguistics are arguably compatible' for the analysis of the scenario. She demonstrates how the narrator relates to Thatcher's 'body image', the way she 'dresses, presents and comports herself', and the assassin 'in counterdistinction, seems to focus on the way in which her body is experienced pre-consciously, that is, the "body schema" of Thatcher'. This results in an exchange of embodied perspectives through which, according to Kukkonen, 'Mantel develops a multi-layered image of sheaths of embodiment' in her story.

Maria Tamboukou also considers someone who is 'embodied as a historical subject that has actually intervened in the social, political and cultural formations of her geographies and times' in order to develop the 'figure of the *narrative persona*'. Despite this active engagement with nineteenth-century revolution, the papers of Désirée Véret-Gay, seamstress, labour activist and writer 'who founded the first feminist newspaper *La Femme Libre*' have not been gathered and her biography remains unwritten. Tamboukou introduces 'the notion of the *narrative persona* as a mode of moving away from the post-structuralist "death of the author" without losing some very important insights that discourse analytics have offered in the field of feminist narratology'. In this essay, Tamboukou looks not at Véret-Gay's political writings but her passionate love letters to Enfantin, leader of the Saint-Simonian movement, and it is here that she 'reconsiders the crucial link between time and narrative'; instead of building a picture of Véret-Gay through study of an archive (the *fond* is the French version), Tamboukou wants to know her in 'the here and now' of her epistolary relationship with Enfantin. Taking her place in a tradition of feminist critics such as Nancy K. Miller and Gayatri Spivak who have incorporated autobiographical revelations into the critical act, Tamboukou asserts her own position ultimately reading her subject as 'an interlocutor with me as a feminist researcher who reads and inserts Désirée's narratives in the archives of feminist history'. Using Deleuze and Guattari's notions of radical immanence, focus on 'moments of being' does not mean that the story she develops of Véret-Gay's *narrative persona* 'represents the real essence or character of who Désirée really was [...] but to point to the limitations of hers and indeed anybody's personal and political narratives to convey the essence of who their author is'. Tamboukou positions the figure of the *narrative persona* as a response to Lanser's 'purely textual' narrator as one who is instead 'both embodied and embedded as a historical subject'.

In my own essay, I read Ali Smith's 2014 *How to be both* in order to reconsider the relationship between visibility and power in the digital age. Smith's formal experimentation in this novel is extreme; it exists in two formats, chance determining whether the reader starts with a Part One set in twenty-first century Cambridge or a Part One set in Renaissance Italy. I argue that Smith's spatial presentation makes us see what is absent in her texts, and that blank spaces in particular can be seen as ways of staging questions of gender and invisibility. Much of Ali Smith's novel can be seen (like its two interchangeable sections) as a refusal of sequence or a spatialisation of time, such as the fresco at the novel's centre, which renders the cycle of the months in a single moment. I propose a formula – a *becoming-simultaneous of narrative sequence* – which functions like Lanser's indeterminate gender voices, to queer the distinction between space and time. The question of vision is central in this argument – of what can be seen and what is unmarked – and I propose that the novel links the question of what cannot be seen to the opacity or invisibility of the future more generally. It does this at the level of the graphic and visual surface of the text, and also in relation to grammatical structures, to develop a connection between power and invisibility which feminism can elucidate as a political power of possibility, of what you can see in relation to what you can become.

The 'unmarked' is also at work in the contributions of Robyn Warhol and Amy Shuman, both of whom identify as 'feminist narratologists', and here combine their different perspectives (Warhol from literary studies and Shuman from linguistic anthropology) to analyse a text which is racially ambiguous. Toni Morrison's only short story 'Recitatif' is 'an experiment in the removal of all racial codes from a narrative about two characters of different races for whom racial identity is crucial'.[21] When they 'combined Amy's interactive, ethnographic method with Robyn's literary, structural analysis ... [they] ... perceived an underlying logic in the story' that neither would have discovered alone. As with my discussions of Smith's fiction, Warhol and Shuman consider the power of prose narrative as a medium in which identity signifiers do not have to exist. Textual production of ambiguous markers, like the textually unmarked, upset social categories by involving readers in a recognition of the principles of their construction. Warhol and Shuman's conclusion that the '"insanity of racism" and the misprision of disability won't be solved by sentimental reconciliations bridging the alterity between the African-American and the white, the not-yet-disabled and the disabled' perfectly represents the impulse behind this edition, and of the theorists who have contributed to it, that writing is a form of social activism.

Notes

1. Brian Richardson, 'Recent Concepts of Narrative and the Narratives of Narrative Theory', *Style*, 34.2 (2000), pp. 168–75, p. 168, p. 172.
2. Susan S. Lanser, 'Toward a Feminist Narratology', in Robyn R. Warhol and Diane Price Herndl (eds), *Feminisms: An Anthology of Theory and Criticism* (Houndmills, Basingstoke: Macmillan Press, 1997), pp. 674–93.

3. Ruth E. Page, *Literary and Linguistic Approaches to Feminist Narratology* (Houndmills, Basingstoke: Palgrave Macmillan, 2006).
4. Judith Roof, *Come As You Are: Sexuality and Narrative* (New York: Columbia University Press, 1996).
5. Greta Olson (ed.), *Current Trends in Narratology* (Berlin and New York: De Gruyter, 2011).
6. Nilli Diengott, 'Narratology and Feminism', *Style*, 22.1 (1988), pp. 42–51, p. 42.
7. Gerald Prince, 'On Narratology: Criteria, Corpus, Context', *Narrative*, 3.1 (1995), pp. 73–84, p. 82.
8. Robyn Warhol and Susan S. Lanser (eds), *Narrative Theory Unbound: Queer and Feminist Interventions* (Columbus: University of Ohio Press, 2015), p. 10.
9. As Prince himself noted in 'On Narratology'.
10. Lanser, 'Toward a Feminist Narratology', p. 676.
11. Ibid., p. 689.
12. Susan S. Lanser, *The Narrative Act: Point of View in Prose Fiction* (Princeton, NJ: Princeton University Press, 1981) and Susan S. Lanser, *Fictions of Authority: Women Writers and Narrative Voice* (Ithaca, NY: Cornell University Press, 1992).
13. Susan S. Lanser, 'Toward (a Queerer and) More (Feminist) Narratology', in Robyn Warhol and Susan S. Lanser (eds), *Narrative Theory Unbound: Queer and Feminist Interventions* (Columbus: University of Ohio Press, 2015), pp. 23–42, p. 30.
14. Patricia Matson, 'The Textual Politics of Virginia Woolf's *Mrs Dalloway*', in Kathy Mezei (ed.), *Ambiguous Discourse: Feminist Narratology and British Women Writers* (Chapel Hill and London: University of North Carolina Press, 1996), pp. 162–86, p. 163.
15. Lanser, 'Toward (a Queerer and) More (Feminist) Narratology', p. 31.
16. Ibid.
17. Nicole Brossard, *The Aerial Letter*, trans. Marlene Wildeman (Toronto: Women's Press, 1988).
18. Warhol and Lanser, *Narrative Theory Unbound*, p. 2.
19. Ibid., p. 10.
20. http://www.lhn.uni-hamburg.de/article/cognitive-narratology-revised-version-uploaded-22-september-2013 [Date accessed: 19 February 2018].
21. Toni Morrison, *Playing in the Dark* (New York: Vintage, 1992), p. xi.

Disclosure statement

No potential conflict of interest was reported by the author.

Funding

This work was supported by the British Academy Small Research Grants [grant number SG121390].

Queering narrative voice

Susan S. Lanser

ABSTRACT
Narrative theory has paid less attention to queer possibilities than narrative itself warrants. This essay takes up the specific subject of narrative voice and asks how it might be 'queered' by considering three distinct meanings of the verb 'to queer'. Seeking as well to establish compatibility between feminist and queer understandings of voice, I explore ways in which both homodiegtetic (first-person) and heterodiegetic (third-person) narrative might take queer forms. Homodiegetic narration may articulate queer sexuality in either implicit or explicit ways; homodiegesis may also resort to strategies of gender ambiguity that render impossible the attribution of a narrator's sex. I also undertake a revisionist engagement with heterodiegetic narration and with the conventional linkages made between the gender of an author and the gender attributed to the narrative voice. I argue that heterodiegetic narration is conventionally queer insofar as it resists sexual determination through textual means. Finally, I call for a queerer understanding of narration while also questioning the value of different definitions of 'queer' for narratological thinking. The essay also proposes an understanding of narrative voice in relation to gender and sexuality that compatibly crosses queer and feminist thought.

> Queering is the covering of a Wall when it is new built, that Rain drive not into it.[1] [Randle Holme, 'Terms Used by the Bricklayer' (1688)]

Not even the *Oxford English Dictionary* can pin down the word 'queer'. Of 'uncertain origin' and shifting syntax, *queer* has described, over half a millennium, the strange and the suspect, the criminally counterfeit, the ill and the inebriate, the disconcerting, the interfering, the merely puzzling, or ridiculous – and all this even before sexual messages seized the term. How fitting, then, that 'queer' continues to slide beneath scholarly fingers even as its usage has become academically ubiquitous. While the *OED* now recognises the adjectival 'queer', if rather elliptically, as describing 'a sexual or gender identity that does not correspond to established ideas of sexuality and gender, especially heterosexual norms', it still does not acknowledge any of the three academic uses of the verb: (1) to make a claim for the non-heteronormative sex, gender, or sexuality of someone or something; (2) to disrupt or deconstruct binary categories of sex, gender, and/or sexuality; and (3) to disrupt or deconstruct any entity by rejecting its categories, binaries, or norms.

Although 'queer' is most often deployed as an adjective, and most often rejected as a noun for its dangers of reifying identities of sexuality and gender, each of its three verbal meanings also enjoys a lively academic life. Scholarly articles claim to queer 'the globally intimate', 'old time religion', 'the countryside', 'maritime archaeology', 'nonverbal communication' 'the workplace', 'the state', 'ecological studies', and in the present case, 'narrative voice'. All three meanings of 'to queer' get evoked in this panoply. The edited collection *Queering the Countryside,* for example, aims to show 'how important rural America can be in the movement to expand equality for LGBT people' – the first meaning – while also leaning playfully on the third: '"Rural America" is strange. Some might even go so far as to say it is queer'.[2] Catriona Mortimer-Sandilands' project of 'Queering Ecocultural Studies' deploys the second definition, by arguing that biological evidence reveals the 'sexually diverse interactions' of non-human organisms.[3] V. Spike Peterson, writing in *Political Geography,* aims at 'Queering the Globally Intimate' through a capacious 'poststructuralist concept' whereby 'queering' means 'deconstructing or "making strange" what appears as "normal" or as the "natural order of things"'.[4]

This incongruous capaciousness of 'queer' extends to the study of narrative. Take, for example, *The Turn of the Screw,* which along with its author Henry James has been more than a little subject to queering. The text's own dozen uses of the word 'queer', while not explicitly sexual, certainly 'resonate', as George Haggerty notes, 'with a hint of transgressive sexuality'.[5] Not surprisingly, then, scholarly investments in queering this novel encompass all three academic meanings: in the first instance, for example, Rictor Norton's claim that Peter Quint is an 'aggressive homosexual'; in the second, Ellis Hansen's argument that sexual ambiguities implicating the entire cast of characters, including the seemingly straight and stolid Mrs Grose; and in the third instance, Eric Savoy's exposure of the baffling obliquity of the entire text.[6] Indeed, what Savoy calls 'queer formalism' – a term that has also entered the visual arts – seems to be grounded in the interactions among all three definitions of 'queer'.[7]

In this piece, I too take up all three meanings of the verb 'to queer' – to transgress normative sexualities, to dismantle sexual fixities, and to dismantle all fixities – to ask what we might gain by bringing any one of them to bear on fictional narrators.[8] In so doing, I also aim to trouble a major assumption in feminist narratology and indeed in my own work: that the binary of gender necessarily figures in the writerly and readerly engagement with narrative voice. I focus specifically on what Genette calls narrative *person* ('who speaks?') because this aspect of narrative form carries mimetic investments worth considering in queer terms. Through this encounter, I want both to trouble the feminist narratology that I have been instrumental in shaping and to suggest ways of addressing the paradoxical mandate to 'queer' gender and yet to affirm gender's significance for apprehending narrative. These efforts, in turn, lead me to interrogate both the relationship between authorial gender and narrative voice on which feminist narratology has tended to rely and the efficacy of narratology itself for a queer politics.

This is not my first foray into queer narratology. In a 1995 essay called 'Sexing the Narrative: Propriety, Desire, and the Engendering of Narratology' that was published in *Narrative*, I responded to Gerald Prince's critique of my 'Toward a Feminist Narratology' by attempting to show the significance of gender to a range of narrative elements from paralipsis to reliability. Ironically for an essay that was advocating attention to gender, however, I chose as my primary example Jeanette Winterson's *Written on the Body* (1992), a novel that brilliantly conceals the gender of its first-person narrator-protagonist. That essay was later adapted for *Ambiguous Discourse: Feminist Narratology and British Women Writers*, edited by Kathy Mezei, with the title 'Queering Narratology'. The unacknowledged tension between these two titles signals the unacknowledged tension between feminist and queer paradigms in the essay itself. Nor did I address this tension in my more recent essay, 'Toward (a Queerer and) More (Feminist) Narratology', published in the volume *Narrative Theory Unbound: Queer and Feminist Intervention* that I coedited with Robyn Warhol in 2015; my strategy there was to couple 'queer and feminist' rather than to probe their potentially fraught relationship. But as Abby Coykendall writes in that same volume, 'combining feminist and queer studies' can 'divorce as much as unite those fields', 'constructing feminism *qua* feminism as not in itself queer, or queer studies as not itself feminist, and thereby rendering the association between them simply an aggregation of one species of activity onto the presumptive alterity of the other'.[9]

In the 1995 essays, I imagined that there might emerge 'a queer narratology in which questions of sexuality become a telescope through which to seek narrative elements not before attended to'.[10] Yet in 2018, and despite work of extraordinary breadth and depth in queer literary studies, queer narratology itself remains underdeveloped, its relationship to feminist narratology underexplored, and its potential contribution to narratology as such unspecified. This foray uses narrative voice as one lens for probing the dissonances between queer and feminist narratologies on the way to configuring a theoretical framework that advances shared aims, and I undertake it the spirit of one of the less common dictionary definitions of queer: to inquire.

'Queer' is not the only queer term at play in this inquiry, however, for 'voice' itself is also potentially queer in my third sense because its use is almost always metaphoric without being recognised as such. Of the five meanings of 'voice' common to textual studies alone, only one is literal: voice as the articulation of sound. More commonly, especially in reference to print, 'voice' signifies an expression of attitude or position ('the voice of reason'; 'a progressive voice'); a category of group identity or collective will ('the voice of the people'); a synonym for style ('a lyrical voice'); or a structural category that describes textual narrators or, Genette puts it, 'the generating instance of narrative discourse'.[11] These meanings also often intermingle in the phrase 'queer voice', which has described phenomena as diverse as a radio show in Houston, an art exhibit in Philadelphia, a writers' conference in Iran, man-to-man love poems of the Spanish Enlightenment, and the film *2001*'s notorious computer HAL.

As a queer-invested scholar, I appreciate this fluid panoply, but as a narratologist I am dissatisfied that 'queer voice' rarely evokes that last, specifically narrative definition that will be my focus here. I want to ask within a narratological framework under what circumstances narrative voice might be considered 'queer'; whether a text that fits some definition of queer might tend towards particular configurations of voice; what the study of narrative voice might gain from its queering; and how queering narrative voice might or might not square with feminist concerns. In this framework, I take 'queer voice' to have one of three meanings corresponding to my three definitions of queer:

(1) a voice belonging to a textual speaker who can be identified as a queer subject by virtue of sex, gender, or sexuality;
(2) a voice that is textually ambiguous or subverts the conventions of sex, gender, or sexuality; and
(3) a voice that confounds the rules for voice itself and thus baffles our categorical assumptions about narrators and narrative.

All of these forms of 'queer voice' are imbricated with conventional narratological categories and especially with the two basic configurations of narrative person that Genette describes when he distinguishes between narrators who are and are not participants in a story world – that is, between homodiegetic ('first-person') narrators who are participants in the story they recount and heterodiegetic ('third-person') narrators who are ontologically separated from the story world. Although Genette reminds us that any narrator has the structural capacity to speak in the first person, his differentiation between homodiegesis and heterodiegesis makes a critical difference to this inquiry because each form implies a different set of grammatical possibilities for inscribing narrative voice.[12] As we will see, each meaning of 'queer' is thus constrained in turn by its narrative environment.

I. Queer orientations: narrators 'in' and 'out'

The most frequently evoked meaning of 'queer voice' – voice belonging to an identifiably queer speaking subject – seems to me narratologically the easiest to accommodate despite its fraught identitarian implications.[13] Insofar as 'queer' designates an explicitly identified *narrating subject* speaking in the first person – usually homodiegetically but potentially also heterodiegetically – queer voice in this sense is analogous to other markers of subject position such as ethnicity, race, class, or nationality that diverge from 'degree zero' cultural assumptions about both narrators and narratees: issues about authority, reliability, and plausibility as well as assumptions about cultural norms. We might take, for example, the head-on first sentences of Moshin Hamid's brilliantly canny *The Reluctant Fundamentalist* (2008), which at once challenges ethnic stereotypes and exploits them: 'Excuse me, sir, may I be of assistance? Ah, I see I have alarmed you. Do not be frightened by my beard: I am a lover of America. ... I see your face has hardened'.[14]

The rub, though, lies with the complication that dramatised narrator-characters who are, say, Pakistani, male and Muslim, like Hamid's Changez – or, female, brown, and British like the unnamed narrator of Zadie Smith's *Swing Time* (2016) – usually identify themselves openly. But queerness, especially in its complex historicity, is probably of all narrative voices the least likely to take an uncoded form. If we are thinking of 'queer voice' in the identitarian sense, then, it would be wise to distinguish between 'out' and 'closeted' narrative voices – that is, between voices sexually self-named and voices open to contestation.[15] This distinction between explicitly and implicitly queer narrators potentially opens major differences not only in narrative practices but in reading practices, and one task for queering narrative theory is to figure out what those practices might be.

Not surprisingly, the openly queer narrator is, with few exceptions, a recent phenomenon. Stephen Macauley's novel *Insignificant Others* (2010), for example, opens like this: 'When I'd learned that Conrad, my partner of eight years, was seeing someone on the side, I wasn't completely surprised.' It takes a few pages to establish with certainty that this narrator is a man: the word 'partner' is suggestive but not definitive, as is the reference to the narrator's 'sagging jowls' on page 3. But once we know that the narrator's name is Richard – on page 7 – we also glean a witty gay male subject addressing a left-leaning, East-Coast-sophisticated, upper-middle-class narratee who is both gay-friendly and gay-aware. Like Zadie Smith's and Moshin Hamid's narrators, Macauley's Richard does not demand much narratological decoding and can be studied intersectionally as one would study other narrators who represent particularised social groups. Openly queer narrators, like all particularised narrators, do raise important questions about how textual speakers characterise themselves *as* queer, whether they seem to be addressing queer or non-queer narratees, and how they construct authority and solicit empathy, and each of these questions, in turn, might be mapped intersectionally by gender, race, class, and other vectors of identity that shape narrative possibilities. Explicitly queer narration also evokes questions about distinctions between public and private narrative situations: when Rita Mae Brown's homodiegetic narrator Molly Bolt (*Rubyfruit Jungle,* 1973) boldly proclaims to an implied reader that she is lesbian, we have moved far from the confessional mode in which a queer character confides sexual secrets only to another character. It would be useful, then, to distinguish a narrator who is 'out' to the extradiegetic narratee who stands in for the reader from a narrator 'out' only to another character within the represented world.

An implicitly queer narrator raises more complex interpretive questions. For instance, the narrator of Sarah Orne Jewett's 1877 novel *Deephaven,* the title of which has itself been read as lesbian code, often speaks of herself and her friend Kate as a 'we', in a strategy that arguably enacts on the level of narration the coupling that cannot explicitly be acknowledged on the level of plot. Particularly interesting are the narrator's extraneous comments, on the one hand, and her ellipses, on the other: practices that together constitute a kind of queering of what can and cannot be said. For example, in an early scene, Helen goes round to Kate's house, makes a point of remarking that she is opening Kate's door with her own latch-key, kisses Kate, and then proclaims that the pair are 'not sentimental girls' and are 'both much averse to indiscriminate kissing', a disavowal that only underscores the import of this particular kiss. Against this excess of information seemingly inconsequential information we get a deep haven of silence about the nightlife of these friends who spend six weeks in a house with a sofa 'broad enough for Kate and [Helen] to lie on together'. The narrator acknowledges that the pair 'breakfasted late' on many a morning but never explains why. This dance of paralepsis (saying too much) and paralipsis (saying too little) illustrates the delicacy of revealing and concealing that epitomises closet narration.

At an even more covert level is the potential queerness, again in this first sense of sexual identity, of the heterodiegetic narrator who shows a particular appreciation for the same-sexed body or a particular understanding of same-sex desire, often in tandem with a tight focalisation on a plausibly queer character. Eve Kosofsky Sedgwick identifies this kind of heterodiegetic, quasi-dramatised narrator in Melville's *Billy Budd,* arguing that he equates 'cognitive mastery of the world in general' with 'mastery of the terms of homoerotic desire' and positing a less comprehending reader with a 'normal nature' through 'indirection'.[16] Similarly, Lawrence Gross argues on grounds of both ideology and affinity that the narrator of Byron's *Don Juan* is 'gay' – if 'closeted' – and that this narrator's 'homoerotic engagement with the hero of his poem, expressed at times through his use of *double entendres*, underscores the poem's endorsement of political and sexual liberty'.[17] If we accept the narrator of Henry James's *Roderick Hudson* as 'male' – a subject to which I will return – then we might likewise construe that narrator as potentially queer in his fascination both with Roderick's own 'altogether extraordinary beauty' and with the 'singular beauty' of his studies of the male nude.[18] In short, we might want to characterise not only homodiegetic but heterodiegetic narrators in relation to signs of heternormativity which, like signs of masculinity and femininity, are of course cultural variables and not fixed norms. Such a move reminds us that narrators, like narratees, can be characterised according to qualities gleaned from their articulated perspectives, frames of knowledge, or focus of attention whether explicitly or only implicitly drawn.[19]

In *The Narrative Act*, I hypothesised that inferences about a heterodiegetic narrator's social identity figure in determining that narrator's authority and presumed reliability. For example, one might reasonably assume on textual evidence that the narrator of Toni Morrison's *Sula* is deeply familiar with African-American history and culture and exposes white supremacy with evocative metaphor and sorrowful irony from the novel's very first sentence: 'In that place, where they tore the nightshade and blackberry patches from their roots to make room for the Medallion City Golf Course, there was once a neighborhood'.[20] In a textual sense, one could plausibly consider this narrator African-American. I am suggesting, in other words, a fuller practice of social identification of narrators on the basis of internal textual signs: the knowledge, values, and assumptions implicit or explicit in the behaviour of the narrating voice, including knowledge, values, and assumptions about sexuality. Such an approach allows us to engage not only homodiegetic but heterodiegetic narrators on the basis of the features that the narrator calls into being and thus also to recognise the deep intersectionality that operates in the readerly processing of narrative voice.

In naming the heterodiegetic narrators of *Deephaven*, *Billy Budd*, *Don Juan*, and *Roderick Hudson* as implicitly queer, and the narrator of *Sula* as implicitly African-American, I have used examples of texts whose *authors* have been so labelled. But this brings me to a major conundrum in theorising narrative voice. Queering has often relied on linkages to putatively queer authors – that is, on presuming that the narrator of a novel authored by a presumably queer writer is therefore presumably queer. As I will discuss more fully below, however, queering narrative voice asks us not to impose social qualities on narrators through external assumptions that cannot be textually sustained. I would thus complicate – okay, queer – my assumptions about the ways in which readers transfer the known social identities of authors to the social identities of narrators even when these identities are unmarked. That is, I want to critique a pervasive practice of tautological reading whereby queer author = queer narrator, and to emphasise instead the value of asking how a queer narrative voice might be coded through formal practices. In so doing, however, I must also reconsider an assumption that has been deeply rooted in my formulations of a feminist narratology: that the gender of an author carries into the gender of an unmarked narrative voice.

II. Genderqueer voices: beyond binaries

I have said that my first category of queer voice, that of identitarian narrators or narrators with queer points of view, bifurcates along the divide of 'out' and 'closeted' – or, more properly, explicitly and implicitly queer. My second category, the sex- or gender-ambiguous narrator, bifurcates along the homodiegetic/heterodiegetic divide, and this time it will be heterodiegetic narration that I want to query by queering my own past work. The homodiegetic narrator who is gender-ambiguous is easy to identify but also relatively uncommon in most language cultures for two potentially related reasons: not only do nearly all cultures operate on gender binaries, but even more importantly, most languages require at least some binary (he/she) or trinary (he/she/it) grammatical gender.[21] I have in mind here those narrative situations in which we have no way to know the sex, gender and/or sexuality of the narrating voice. I have already mentioned Jeanette Winterson's *Written on the Body* (1992), which figured prominently in my 1995 work and which exploits the relative gender neutrality of the English first-person pronoun to create an entire novel whose narrator-protagonist cannot be pinned down in either gender or sexuality. British mystery writer Sarah Caudwell also pulls off this ambiguity across four detective novels (1981–2000) that feature the ungendered first-person narrator-sleuth Hilary Tamar, 'an Oxford don' of 'equivocal sex', as Caudwell herself put it. Maureen Duffy's *Love Child* (1971) likewise features a sexually ambiguous child narrator, Kit, preoccupied with their mother's love affair with a person who is also sexually ambiguous. Anne Garréta's *Sphinx* (1986) provides an even more exceptional instance because it is composed in the more grammatically challenging language of French and because it genders both the first-person narrator-character and the third-person co-protagonist A***.[22] The rarity of such gender-ambiguous narrator-protagonists in Western fiction, in contrast to the frequency of gender-ambiguous first-person voices in Western poetry, arguably underscores the so-called Cartesian split that allows the mind or soul to remain ungendered (the lyric voice) but insists on the corporeality of social action (the voice of narrative).

Another form of homodiegetic narration, the 'we' narrative, can also take a queer turn. In *Fictions of Authority*, I proposed the term 'communal voice' to describe 'practices that articulate either a collective voice or a collection of voices that share narrative authority'.[23] I identified a 'simultaneous' form of 'we' narration in which the narrator is a kind of amalgam of a set of individuals in a way that I would now call unnatural. As Monika Fludernik reminds us in a recent essay on the collective in the narrative, 'the imaginative affordances of fiction' can be deployed to emphasise either 'unity and solidarity' or 'the lack thereof', not least because 'in fiction the semantics of *we* often remain deliberately vague'.[24] This 'we' can bridge more and less inclusive groups, remain fuzzy in its referential limits, and even cross or combine temporalities. Although in *Fictions of Authority* I concentrated on all-female communal voices, a 'we-narrator' can of course encompass both male and female characters or characters whose gender is not specified and thus create a gender-inclusive or genderqueer collective voice. Natalya Bekhta argues for we-narrative as a separate form 'whose nature it is to possess *collective* epistemological, perspectival, and other qualities and thus create new narrative "rules"'.[25] Bekhta's primary example is Joshua Ferris's clever *Then We Came to the End* (2007), in which the collective subject is a group of workers at an advertising agency who narrate not only actions but feelings and values, all in the name of the group. Individuals are referred to only in the third person, as characters, even when they also form part of the group. Sometimes the 'we' does divide into subgroups like 'some of us' and 'most of us', but without setting apart any singular 'I' on the narrative level. The collective subject as constructed in Ferris's novel speaks for both male and female characters of diverse ethnicities and backgrounds (including at least one gay man). In articulating a plural consciousness irreducible to one sex or gender, this we-narration affords a kind of proto-utopian exercise in which gender, race, sexuality, and other conventional social classifications fail to signify discreet features; instead, the collective is forged by shared circumstance and intentional community.

In dramatic contrast to the rare gender ambiguity of homodiegetic narrators, the heterodiegetic gender-ambiguous narrator – that is, the narrator whose gender is never specified – is so common as to constitute the norm. That is, heterodiegetic narrators are rarely self-dramatised by gender after the manner, say, of Fielding's narrator in *Tom Jones*, who evokes his status as 'gentleman' in the novel's first sentence. In the more common case, we *attribute* gender – and also, I suggest, attribute normative sexuality – to heterodiegetic voices that arguably do not carry it. Consider the narrator of any typical heterodiegetic novel, and you will probably be hard-pressed to ascribe sex to its narrator on textual grounds. Yet from my first narratological publication, *The Narrative Act: Point of View in Prose Fiction*, I have assumed that all narrators have gender and argued that the gender of a heterodiegetic narrator derives from the gender of the paratextually inscribed author, though I did speculate that the authority conventionally given to male voices might override the link between authorial and narratorial sex in the case of a woman writer. This hypothesis underwrote what both David Richter and Manfred Jahn dubbed 'Lanser's rule': the convention that in the absence of internal clues to the narrator's gender, readers attribute the gender of the author, by default, to the narrating voice.[26] But even if this postulate accurately describes some or even most reading practices, we must acknowledge that heterodiegetic gender is usually not a textual property but a socially conditioned inference. We might also recognise such readerly behaviour as historically contingent: in the late 1970s, when I wrote the dissertation that became *The Narrative Act,* I found instances of scholarship that designated the narrator of *Pride and Prejudice* as 'he'. Studies published in the twenty-first century, by contrast, consistently refer to the narrator as 'she'.

What was called 'Lanser's rule' did not go unquestioned even when I proposed it. As Jahn notes, Jonathan Culler recognised in *Framing the Sign* that narrators may be of indeterminate identity and that the author–narrator link is conceptually vulnerable. Marie-Laure Ryan's essay 'Cyberage Narratology' likewise argued that my universal attribution of gender to the 'impersonal third-person narrator' was a case of 'literalizing the metaphor' of voice, and thus attributing 'human embodiment' to entities with 'superhuman omniscience'. Ryan also objected to what she saw as my 'theoretical attempt to legislate over [her] own act of imagination by imposing' on her a 'needlessly specific representation'.[27] One might also ask how 'Lanser's rule' could be applied to novels whose authorship is uncertain, anonymous, or pseudonymous. What gender did Victorian readers – or do readers today – confer on the narrator of *Middlemarch*: the gender of George Eliot or the gender of Mary Anne Evans? Robyn Warhol recognises the problem when she writes in *Gendered Interventions* that 'assigning a gender to Eliot's narrators is no straightforward task', effectively queering Eliot's narrators *avant la lettre*, all the more as these narrators exhibit qualities that Warhol's framework would mark as both masculine and as feminine.[28] The problem with 'Lanser's rule', in short, is not only its claim that readers invariably confer gender where the text does not mark it, but its insistence that they what they confer is what we would now identify as narrative 'cisgender' – a state in which the author's and the heterodiegetic narrator's genders both coincide with a normative body. And the rule insists on such gender agreement on the basis of very limited empirical knowledge concerning how readers read.

There were good reasons to posit the association of gender and voice in my work towards a feminist narratology, and some of these reasons persist. To the extent that social and cultural authority remain masculine, 'Lanser's rule' insists on authorising specifically female voices and thereby helps to re-gender authority itself. The rule also reminds us to be aware of both implicit and explicit markers of a narrator's gender. But it is equally important to acknowledge and theorise the pervasiveness of ungendered heterodiegetic narration in novels by both women and men. Most of us are probably familiar with the undergraduates who say, 'in this novel, *it* says'; perhaps this practice of desexing voice by way of the neutral pronoun 'it' is not simply a sign of ignorance, as I have admittedly lamented, but a recognition that the godlike narrator is also a disembodied one – a neuter, a cyborg, a HAL. (In this sense, the 'it' resembles the neutral pronoun 'they' currently in chosen by persons who reject the binary of he or she.) Rather than assigning gender to a narrator on the basis of an author's identity, we might explore how *normative* sexual indeterminacy opens heterodiegetic narration to the breadth, fluidity and instability of voice, to its potential to be everywhere or nowhere, aligned through focalisation with a single textual body or with or myriad bodies in turn.

Leaving voice unmarked in this manner also exposes the potential fallacy of making any conventional linkage between author and narrator and thus transferring identities across ontological boundaries instead of relying on textual indices of gender as of other social indices. I mentioned earlier that most of the narrators that scholars claim to be queer happen to be narrators whose *authors* are known for or suspected of homosexuality: Byron and James, Melville and Jewett, Duffy and Winterson. Starting instead with textual features opens a far larger corpus of authors to the possibility of queer practices, as signs not of their own queerness but of the potential queerness of narration itself. We might also want to acknowledge how little we know about how actual readers produce narrative gender in the absence of textual markings, and put hypotheses like 'Lanser's rule' to the empirical test.

Is queering narrative voice in this way a detriment to a feminist narratology? I think not, so long as we also refuse to mark unmarked authority as masculine or heterosexual or cis-gendered and double down on those instances when voice *is* gendered whether hetero- or homodiegetically so as to expose and interrogate the critical role that gender plays in constructing virtually all societies and in shaping their literatures. In contrast to the gendered and heteronormative history of most societies, the ungendered – which is to say ambigendered – narrator reminds us that fictional narration is a semiotic wonder not always reducible to the corporeality that normatively constrains both historical authors and fictional characters.

I noted earlier that voice is one of the formal elements that carries deep mimetic investments on the part of readers; queering narrative voice would emphasise the freedom of the verbal text to imagine a world beyond gender that resists conventional categories and conventional hierarchies of masculinity and femininity: 'queering' in this sense is indeed the protective cover for a newly built wall that my epigraph suggests. In an essay recently published in *Futures of Comparative Literature*, I argued for a 'strategic duality that recognizes histories of dominance and difference without accepting identity categories as essential, permanent, or predictive'.[29] One glory of unmarked narrative voice is precisely its resistance to identity categories or, conversely, its canny and tantalising ability to play with them – queer in the second definition and tapping into the third. As Marie-Laure Ryan argues, the ability to 'morph' by following and effectively inhabiting multiple characters is 'one of the most remarkable features of third-person narration with variable focalization'; pragmatically speaking, such a variability is 'impossible', yet readers routinely accept its use.

III. Queering it all?

Which brings me to the third meaning of 'queer', the definition that encompasses acts that baffle or deconstruct binaries of any sort, quite apart from sexuality or gender. We might consider 'queering' in this sense metalepsis, the condition that John Pier describes as 'a paradoxical contamination between the world of the telling and the world of the told' and that Shlomith Rimmon-Kenan sees as 'undermin[ing] the separation between narration and story'.[30] We might want to 'queer' the narrative transgression of *Madame Bovary*, whose opening sentence – 'we were in class when the head-master came in' – promises an eye-witness narrator who dissolves after one chapter into an omniscient voice. We might 'queer' free indirect discourse, since it is often elusively dual or even multiple in voice so that it becomes impossible fully to separate the narrator's words or implications from those of the character; in some instances, it is simply impossible to determine whose – or even how many – voices blend into a single narrated utterance.[31] The irreducible ambiguity that 'queer' conveys might help to restrain narratology's procrustean tendency to resolve the unresolvable, to recognise, as Virginia Woolf's *To the Lighthouse* puts it, that 'nothing [is] simply one thing'.

These narrative transgressions have nothing to do with gender and sexuality beyond the claim that gender is the foundational binary of binaries. Is there any value, then, to using 'queer' to designate all deconstructive practices, even those practices that might be productive for queer feminist thought? Some theorists argue that the expansive 'queer' dilutes the significance of the sex/gender nexus around which the first two meanings are organised; others argue that the expansive 'queer' carries a valuable in-your-face positivity of 'queer' or promotes a causal relationship between queer genders or sexualities and other transgressive practices. While my own preference is for the more restrictive use, it may be useful to ask whether queer writers in the first or second sense have been particularly innovative in their use of transgressive or deconstructive forms. D. A. Miller argues as much when he claims in *Bringing Out Roland Barthes* that formal innovation may be the displaced project of the queer author who cannot speak her name; Eve Kosofsky Sedgwick makes a similar implication about the gothic. This logic also underwrites E. L. McCallum's attribution of 'queer rhythm' to Gertrude Stein's sentences and to her argument that 'time in Stein's *The Making of Americans* unquestionably has something queer about it'.[32] And narratologists might wonder whether it is accidental that so many modernist innovators in the practice of FID – Henry James, Virginia Woolf, Dorothy Richardson, Marcel Proust, Colette, Djuna Barnes, Katharine Mansfield, and perhaps James Joyce – were queer or queerish folks. In this context, it is worth recalling that the texts on which Barthes and Genette expend their own narratological energies, respectively *Sarrazine* and *A la recherche*, are queer texts. Genette never acknowledges that queerness in his *Discours du récit*, and Barthes does so only obliquely in *S/Z*, yet both lay groundwork that narrative theorists can appropriate towards queerer ends.

Or so I hope. In critical responses included in *Narrative Theory Unbound*, Abby Coykendall and Martin J. Ponce expose the subordination of feminist and queer into adjectival modifiers of the volume's anchor terms 'narrative' and 'narratology'. Coykendall rightly charges that work in cultural studies has focused on narrative – for example, in the work of Homi Bhabha, Judith Butler, Eve Kosofsky Sedgwick, indeed Michel Foucault – without receiving due recognition as narrative *theory*, while Ponce points to 'the incongruous intellectual histories and political commitments' that inhibit 'reciprocal engagements across queer, feminist, and narrative theory' and underscores the tension between narrative theory's tendencies of 'imperialist appropriation' and its 'genuine commitment to accounting for and historicizing' different practices. Mostly challengingly, Ponce calls on narratology not simply to 'bring renewed attention to issues of narrative form in feminist and queer expressive cultures' but to consider the ways that narratology itself might 'be impacted and reshaped by the urgencies presented by feminist and queer studies and politics'.[33] It will be up to scholars like Coykendall and Ponce to judge whether this particular foray into 'queering narrative voice' perpetuates narratology's failings or promotes a textual practice that is both feminist and queer.

Notes

1. Randle Holme, *The Academy of Armory, or, a Storehouse of Armory and Blazon* (Chester: Printed for the author, 1688), p. 261; cited in the *Oxford English Dictionary* under the entry for 'queer'.

    I thank Daniella Gati for her productive response to an early version of this essay and Abby Coykendall for her extensive engagement with the penultimate draft.

2. Colin R. Johnson, Brian J. Gilley, and Mary Gray, 'Introduction', in Johnson Gray and Gilley (eds.), *Queering the Countryside: New Frontiers in Rural Queer Studies* (New York: New York University Press, 2016), pp. 4–5.
3. Catriona Mortimer-Sandilands, 'Queering Ecocultural Studies', *Cultural Studies*, 22 (2008), pp. 458–60.
4. V. Spike Peterson, 'Toward Queering the Globally Intimate', *Political Geography*, 56 (January 2017), pp.114–16 (p. 114).
5. See George Haggerty, *Queer Gothic* (Urbana and Chicago: University of Illinois Press, 2006), pp. 134–5.

6. See Rictor Norton, *Gay History and Literature* (http://rictornorton.co.uk/henjames.htm); Ellis Hansen, 'Screwing with Children in Henry James', *GLQ*, 9 (2003), pp. 367–91; and Eric Savoy, 'The Jamesian Turn: A Primer on Queer Formalism', in Kimberly C. Reed and Peter G. Beidler (eds.), *Approaches to Teaching Henry James's Daisy Miller and the Turn of the Screw* (New York: The Modern Language Association, 2005), pp. 132–42.
7. For a discussion of queer formalism in visual art, see Jennifer Doyle and David Getsy, 'Queer Formalisms', *Art Journal Open* (2014). http://artjournal.collegeart.org/?p=4468.
8. I focus exclusively on print narrative because of the different – and indeed more literal – capacities of narrative voice in performative media such as film, theatre, and storytelling.
9. Abby Coykendall, 'Towards a Queer Feminism; Or, Feminist Theories and/as Queer Narrative Studies', in Robyn Warhol and Susan S. Lanser (eds.), *Narrative Theory Unbound: Queer and Feminist Interventions* (Columbus: Ohio State University Press, 2015), pp. 325–33 (p. 326). Coykendall makes a more radical critique than that which I am addressing here; she argues that when either 'queer' or 'feminist' is used to *modify* 'narrative theory', narrative theory remains the anchor that subordinates the other term.
10. Susan S. Lanser, 'Sexing the Narrative: Propriety, Desire, and the Engendering of Narratology', *Narrative*, 3.1 (1995), pp. 85–94.
11. Gérard Genette, *Narrative Discourse: An Essay in Method*, trans Jane Lewin (Ithaca, NY: Cornell U Press, 1980), p. 213.
12. Genette, *Narrative Discourse*, p. 244. I say *a* rather than *the* story world because characters in one story world can, of course, become narrators at another diegetic level. As Genette puts it, 'the real question is whether or not the narrator can use the first person to designate one of his characters' or, instead, is 'absent from the story he tells' (p. 244). The distinction I have in mind here is that between narrators who are both extradiegetic and heterodiegetic and narrators who are homodiegetic *or* who narrate heterodiegetically as characters within a first-level diegesis.
13. While I recognize that any definition of queer subjectivity will be contested, I take 'queer' to encompass the range of sexual and gender identities conventionally implicated under the 'LGBTQUIA' acronym. I recognize that this range already brings together the conflicting fixities of words such as 'gay' and 'lesbian' with the openness of 'queer' itself. It is difficult to theorize a queer narratology, or indeed to advance any practical politics, without accepting the terminological dissonances at work in the acronym itself. I recognize as well the historically and culturally contingent nature of this entire category and the subject position to which it refers.
14. Mohsin Hamid, *The Reluctant Fundamentalist* (New York: Harcourt, 2007), pp. 1–2.
15. The (expanding) acronym currently encompasses lesbian, gay, bisexual, transgender, intersex, queer, and asexual identity categories.
16. Eve Kosofsky Sedgwick, *Epistemology of the Closet* (Berkeley: University of California Press, 1990), p. 98.
17. Jonathan David Gross, '"One Half What I Should Say": Byron's Gay Narrator in *Don Juan*', *European Romantic Review*, 9.3 (1998), pp. 323–49 (p. 323).
18. Henry James, *Roderick Hudson* [1875] (Harmondsworth: Penguin, 1986), pp. 64, 72.
19. On the characteristics of narratees, arguably applicable as well to narrators, see Lanser, 'A Prince for All Seasons, with Notes Toward the Delineation of a New Yorker Narratee', *Narrative*, 22 (2014), pp. 289–97.

20. Toni Morrison, *Sula* (New York: Knopf, 1973), p. 3.
21. All Semitic and Indo-European languages carry some form of grammatical gender. The extent of this gendering ranges from English, which requires gender identification only in third-person pronouns, to European languages like French, where third-person plural pronouns and adjectives are gendered, through Hebrew and Arabic, which genders not only pronouns and adjectives but also verbs. Turkic languages (Finnish, Turkish, Hungarian), Chinese, and Japanese are among languages that do not gender grammatically.
22. Ernaux's and Winterson's brilliant achievements pose challenges for those who have translated the book into languages more gender-inflected than English or French.
23. Susan Lanser, *Fictions of Authority: Women Writers and Narrative Voice* (Ithaca, NY: Cornell UP, 1992), p. 21.
24. Monika Fludernik, 'Toward a Poetics of the Collective in Narrative', 155–6, *Narrative*, 25.3 (May 2017), pp. 139–63.
25. Natalya Bekhta, 'We-Narratives: The Distinctiveness of Collective Narration', *Narrative*, 25.3 (May 2017), pp. 170, 176–7.
26. See especially Manfred Jahn, *Narratology: A Guide to the Theory of Narrative* (University of Köln, 2017), http://www.uni-koeln.de/~ame02/pppp.htm, p. 34.
27. Marie-Laure Ryan, 'Cyberage Narratology: Computers, Metaphor, and Narrative', in David Herman (ed.), *Narratologies: New Perspectives on Narrative Analysis* (Columbus: Ohio State University Press, 1999), pp. 113–41, p. 136.
28. Robyn Warhol, *Gendered Interventions: Narrative Discourse in the Victorian Novel* (New Brunswick, NJ: Rutgers University Press, 1989), p. 115.
29. Susan S. Lanser, 'Comparatively Lesbian: Queer/Feminist Theory and the Sexuality of History', in Ursula K. Heise et al. (eds.), *Futures of Comparative Literature: ACLA State of the Discipline Report* (London and New York: Routledge, 2017), pp. 92–7, p. 95.
30. See John Pier, 'Metalepsis', *Living Handbook of Narratology*, http://wikis.sub.uni-hamburg.de/lhn/index.php/Metalepsis; and Shlomith Rimmon-Kenan, *Narrative Fiction: Contemporary Poetics* (London: Routledge, 1983/2002), p. 93.
31. In Katherine Mansfield's 'The Garden Party', to take one quick example, one invariably comes up against confounding passages irreducible to any one vocal entity, like the one that refers to the 'little mean' brown cottages that 'were far too near', and 'the greatest possible eyesore', of which 'the very smoke coming out of their chimneys was poverty-stricken'.
32. E. L. McCallum, 'Stein und *Zeit*', in E. L. McCallum and Mikko Tuhkanen (eds.), *Queer Times, Queer Becomings* (Albany: State University of New York Press, 2011), pp. 233–56.
33. Coykendall, 'Towards a Queer Feminism', p. 329 and Martin Joseph Ponce, 'Queer/Feminist/Narrative: On the Limits of Reciprocal Engagement', in Robyn Warhol and Susan S. Lanser (eds.), *Narrative Theory Unbound: Queer and Feminist Interventions* (Columbus: Ohio State University Press, 2015), pp. 334–9, p. 335.

Disclosure statement

No potential conflict of interest was reported by the author.

Rethinking the subject in feminist research: narrative personae and stories of 'the real'

Maria Tamboukou

ABSTRACT

In this paper, I discuss the question of 'the death of the subject' within feminist narratology and beyond. In doing this, I bring forward the notion of the 'narrative persona', a configuration that refers to the writing of feminist genealogies by drawing on women's auto/biographical narratives. The narrative personae of my inquiries emerge from Deleuze and Guattari's philosophy and Arendt's political thought: they are taken as conceptual and aesthetic figures, who narrate and act and whose stories create a scene for dialogic exchanges, communication, understanding, ethical responsibility and action. In fleshing out the concept of the narrative persona, I draw on my research with women workers' narratives particularly focusing on Désirée Véret-Gay, the seamstress who founded the first feminist newspaper *La Femme Libre* in nineteenth-century France. Her political writings in the form of letters, petitions and journal articles have become a significant body in the archives of feminist history. But although she lived a fully active political life she did not reveal much about her inner thoughts and passions, with the exception of a few letters that I will discuss in this paper entering into the dialogue of her epistolary discourse.

'I was born on April 4, 1810'[1] Désirée Véret-Gay (1810–1891) wrote to the old friend and lover of her youth Victor Considerant,[2] on 21 June 1890 from Place St Gudule in Brussels. Her 12 letters to Considerant, sent between 1890 and 1891, are 'among the most beautiful and moving documents in the whole Considerant archive'[3] historian Jonathan Beecher has noted in his extended studies of the Fourierist social movement. In this essay, I look at Désirée's[4] letters and political writings in an attempt to sketch a pen-portrait of a leading figure in the first autonomous feminist movement in nineteenth-century France. Despite her prominence in the history of Western feminism, as well as her active involvement in the European revolutionary movements in the second half of the nineteenth century, Désirée's papers have never been assembled, recorded or organised, while her biography has yet to be written.

Désirée was born and grew up in turbulent times marked by fierce political uprisings, constitutional changes, radical economic development and intense labour activism. As a young proletarian girl working in the Parisian garment industry, she was among those workers who were involved in the European romantic socialist movements: Saint-Simonianism and Fourierism in France and Owenism in Britain. These movements and their influence on the political formations of modernity have been the object of numerous studies both in French and English historiographies.[5] It was their egalitarian position vis-à-vis women, their focus on social issues and questions, as well as their pragmatic approaches to the idea of a new organisation of work beyond class and gender divisions of labour that made their ideas so appealing to young proletarian women workers of the early industrial period. Looking back at her life, while living in solitude and almost blind in Brussels, Désirée would remember the revolutionary activities of her youth and her admiration for the followers of the Saint-Simonian ideas:

> I was searching the light and a thick veil was hiding it from my eyes. However, I never despaired, I had faith [...] in a different world [and] here I am in this new world, the veil has fallen [...] my eyes have opened, I have seen a beautiful picture in the future.[6]

But disillusioned by the way the Saint-Simonian hierarchy marginalised women, despite the egalitarian principles of their doctrine,[7] Désirée detached herself from the movement as early as 1832: 'There is different work to be done. For me all social questions depend on women's freedom'[8] she wrote in *La Femme Nouvelle*, the feminist newspaper that she had founded with her comrade and fellow worker Marie-Reine Guindorf only months before, in August 1832. It was around this time that Désirée turned to Fourierism and in spring 1833 she decided to move to London where she worked as a seamstress for almost two years. Her letters to Charles Fourier reveal that she did not enjoy her life in England: 'My nature has been broken and twisted by civilization. There is in me a chaos I cannot clarify; the longer I live, the more incomprehensible I find myself'[9] she wrote from 37 Duke St, Manchester Square in London.

Despite her difficulties in England, Désirée got involved in the Owenite circles and worked closely with Anna Wheeler,[10] 'who was like a second mother to me'.[11] On returning to France in 1834 she worked in Dieppe first in the women's clothing industry and then in Paris again, while remaining active in the Fourierist and Owenite circles. It was during this time that she had a brief affair with Considerant:

> I guessed from the beginning your defects and your qualities and in spite of myself I loved everything about you. Nothing has escaped my memory: from

your arrival at Paris in 1832 and your visit with Fugère up until the last time I saw you in 1837 at Robert Owen's rooms in the Hôtel de l'Angleterre.[12]

In 1837 Désirée married Jules Gay, who was Owen's translator and close follower, and had two sons, Jean in 1838 and Owen in 1842. Together they tried to found an infant school at ChâtillonsousBagneux in 1840; the school was to be based on Owen's pedagogical model of educating children in freedom,[13] but the project did not succeed in the end, perhaps it was too much ahead of its time.

Désirée immersed herself in labour activism and later in the fierce politics of the February 1848 revolution.[14] Together with Jeanne Deroin she contributed to the daily newspaper *La Voix des Femmes* between March and June 1848. She then became editor of the *Politique des Femmes*, which only published two issues and was closed down in the aftermath of the June 1848 uprising. After a second attempt to run the school at ChâtillonsousBagneux in 1848, Désirée resumed her work as a dressmaker and opened an atelier in the Parisian fashion street par excellence, rue de la Paix – a successful enterprise as her 'honourable mention' in the 1855 Paris international exhibition, testifies.[15] However, in 1864 she had to emigrate once more as her husband's editorial activities were considered unlawful: they faced a series of censorship attacks and they finally chose exile to avoid imprisonment. After a short time wandering in Europe, including Belgium, Switzerland and Italy, they eventually settled down in Brussels. During this period she got involved in the international labour movement and served as the temporary president of the women's section in the central committee of the First Workers' International, held in Geneva in 1866,[16] while in 1868 she published the book *Éducation rationnelle de la première enfance: manuel à l'usage des jeunes mères* in Geneva and London.[17] Her ideas and impressions about labour politics in general and Belgium in particular are vividly expressed in her letter to Considerant:

> The movement seen up close here as a whole, in this little Belgian country, is a curious thing to study insofar as it is a mixture of enthusiasm, sentiment and above all, the positivity that typifies the Belgian character [...] Once upon a time I used to say jokingly that Belgium was a mere baby. Now it is entering its virile passionate stage.[18]

Désirée must have died sometime after July 1891, the date of her last extant letter, but we will never know for sure. It is also from her extant letters that we have learnt that she had outlived her husband and her two sons: 'I have a free spirit and I am independent due to the little fortune that my beloved sons and my husband have left me'[19] she wrote to Considerant. Although the seamstress who signed as Jeanne-Désirée, Désirée Véret, Désirée Gay and also Désirée Véret, veuve Gay, lived a fully active political life she did not reveal much about her inner thoughts and passions, with the exception of a few letters. Her political writings in the form of petitions, journal articles and letters have become a significant body in the archives of feminist history that cannot be restricted within the boundaries of Saint-Simonianism, Fourierism, Owenism, utopian socialism, or any other labels that have been attached to the European social movements of the nineteenth century. As I have argued elsewhere, it was her entanglement in the material conditions of her work as a seamstress that created conditions of possibility for her political ideas and practices to emerge and unfold, making connections with, but not reduced to the ideas and discourses of nineteenth-century romantic socialism.[20] But apart from some biographical elements that I have traced across her documents and have roughly sketched above, is it possible to know more about Désirée, as indeed about many figures in the history of feminism? This is the question that I want to explore in this paper, by introducing the notion of the *narrative persona* as a mode of moving away from the post-structuralist 'death of the author' without losing some very important insights that discourse analytics have offered in the field of feminist narratology. The paper unfolds in three parts: following this introductory section, I give an overview of the philosophical underpinnings of the notion of the *narrative persona* and finally I look at Désirée's letters as traces of the historicity of her subject positions and as components in the assemblage of her desires, her words and her actions.

Conceptual and methodological entanglements

In configuring Désirée as a *narrative persona*, I have followed Deleuze and Guattari's juxtaposition of *conceptual personae* in philosophy and *aesthetic figures* in art, as discussed in their last collective work, *What is Philosophy?*.[21] 'Philosophy constantly brings conceptual personae to life'[22] Deleuze and Guattari have suggested: the Socrates in Plato, the Dionysus in Nietzsche, the Idiot in Descartes becoming their exemplars for the most well-known conceptual personae in the history of philosophy. *Conceptual personae* become the subjects of philosophical enunciations, 'the becoming or the subject of a philosophy on a par with the philosopher'.[23] The philosopher speaks through his/her conceptual persona, keeping a critical distance from what is being said and from the subject of enunciation. It is a third person, the *conceptual persona*, not the philosopher, that says I, since there is always a multiplicity of enunciations and subjects in the work of philosophy. In this light, Deleuze and Guattari explain that

> the conceptual persona is not the philosopher's representative but, rather, the reverse: the philosopher is only the envelope of his principal conceptual persona and of all the other personae who are the intercessors [*intercesseurs*], the real subjects of his philosophy. Conceptual personae are the philosopher's 'heteronyms', and the philosopher's name is the simple pseudonym of his personae.[24]

While philosophy invents *conceptual personae*, art creates *aesthetic figures*: 'the great aesthetic figures of thought and the novel but also of painting, sculpture and music produce affects that surpass ordinary affections and perceptions, just as concepts go beyond everyday opinions'.[25] Many of us share Mrs Dalloway's love of flowers, admire *Les Demoiselles d'Avignon* and are carried away by Carmen's passionate dance and singing. The way we connect with such aesthetic figures in literature, paintings and opera is different to our imaginary dialogues with Socrates or Dionysus. *Conceptual personae* and *aesthetic figures*, 'may pass into one another, in either direction'[26] but should not be conflated, as Deleuze and Guattari note, since 'the former are the powers of concepts, and the latter are the powers of affects and percepts'.[27]

Emerging from a genealogical line of politically active seamstresses that shook France in the long durée of the nineteenth century, Désirée is configured as a *narrative persona* on an analytical plane wherein I have made connections between 'the powers of concepts' and 'the powers of percepts and affects' as forces erupting from her letters and political writings. In this context, Désirée becomes a mediator through whom narrative as philosophy mobilises thinking and narrative as a feeling for the world produces affects. Her letter to Enfantin, the leader of the Saint-Simonian movement in August 1832 is a powerful narrative wherein the philosophical concept of love as a force of life, and the writer's feelings for the addressee, are forcefully expressed in their entanglement:

> Enfantin [...] I can speak to you freely today because my actions are consistent with my words and soon the world will know me as you yourself first came to know me [...] I enter a totally new path [...] I want to talk about feelings, I have always feared love because I did not have faith in the morality of men [...] you have upset and destroyed my dreams, you have not given me enough to satisfy me but you have given me enough to make me desire more. [...] it is because of you that I can love this world [...][28]

My reading of Désirée's passionate letters draws on a conceptualisation of narrative as force. Such an approach reconsiders the crucial link between time and narrative and particularly challenges the almost canonical association of narratives with sequence. An image of time as duration is the philosophical underpinning of this take on narrative analysis, an interest in how narratives create meaning through forcefully exposing and enlightening the unrepeatable boldness, extremity and transgression of Virginia Woolf's 'moments of being'.[29] To put it simply in reading Désirée's letters I am more interested in how her portrait is being drawn in 'the here and now' of her epistolary relationship with Enfantin, rather than in how her narrative identity or character is constituted through the emplotment of sequential events in her life. In this light it is Désirée as a *narrative persona* that I enter in conversation with, responding to the concepts and affects that erupt from the lines of her letters. As a *narrative persona*, the letter writer becomes 'a third person': she cannot be conflated with 'the real Désirée', since she is always, already impossible to pin down, but still she becomes an interlocutor with me as a feminist researcher who reads and inserts Désirée's narratives in the archives of feminist history.

There are interesting connections here with Susan Lanser's pithy observation that 'feminist critics tend to be more concerned with characters than with any other aspect of narrative and to speak of characters largely as if they were persons'.[30] Lanser's important intervention that has shaped the field of feminist narratology has pointed to the figure of 'the narrator' and the possibility and indeed necessity of discerning distinct voices and diverse narratees within multiple narrative levels. While Lanser's 'narrator' is purely textual, however, despite 'the social poetics' and 'narrative circumstances' of her voice, the figure of the *narrative persona* is both embodied and embedded as a historical subject that has actually intervened in the social, political and cultural formations of her geographies and times.

It is in addressing the *narrative persona* as a historical subject that I have turned to Arendt's configuration of 'the persona' on political grounds. As Arendt notes in her book *On Revolution*, the roots of the persona are to be found in ancient drama wherein it has a twofold function: (a) as a mask disguising the actor in theatre and (b) as a device that although disguising would allow the voice of the actor to sound through.[31] If we follow the historicity of the notion, however, in Roman times, the persona passes from the theatre to the legal realm where it means a legal personality, a Roman citizen and not any natural person. So what I take from Arendt is the figure of 'the persona' as acting/performing in the public sphere, while at the same time bearing rights that I, as a feminist narrative researcher recognise and honour. In doing so I make connections between Arendt's radical phenomenology and Deleuze and Guattari's philosophical insights on radical immanence. Arendt asserts that human beings appear to each other 'in such a way that nobody is ever the same as anyone else who ever lived, lives or will live'.[32] Her unique take of plurality goes hand in hand with 'incarnated singularities', thus radicalising the phenomenological tradition she emerges from, as Adriana Cavarero has suggested.[33] Deleuze and Guattari's radical immanence, the assertion that nothing ever has to go outside itself to realise itself, creates conceptual personae and aesthetic figures that decentre subjective thought and creation while viewing the subject 'as a singular complexity [...] in terms of a connection that takes place between self and others', as Rosi Braidotti has argued.[34] I am aware of such conjunctions and disjunctions in my philosophical toolbox, my overall approach, however, is to read diffractively across philosophical traditions when the insights I bring together can become consistent within specific analytical contexts and problems.

In this light, the notion of the *narrative persona* in my analytics is taken as a conceptual and aesthetic figure, who acts and whose story we can follow in the pursuit of meaning and understanding. But the fact that we follow the story of the *narrative persona* does not necessarily mean that this story represents the real essence or character of who Désirée really was. This is not to deny that she was a real person, but to point to the limitations of hers and indeed anybody's personal and political narratives to convey the essence of who their author is. As Arendt has aptly put it: 'nothing entitles us to assume that [man] has a nature or essence in the same sense as other things'.[35] But the lack of essence does not necessarily lead to the death of the subject. While rejecting essence, Arendt theorises human existence, 'life itself, natality and mortality, worldliness, plurality and the earth',[36] but here again she emphasises the fact that we are not reducible to the conditions of human existence. Instead of a unified and autonomous subject, there are nomadic passages and subject positions that the narrative personae of my inquiries take up and move between, while writing and/or visualising stories of the self. Moreover, it is through their stories that certain concepts, ideas and events can be expressed, rehearsed and dramatised so that their enactment can create a scene for dialogic exchanges, communication, understanding and action.

Further considered within the legal dimension of the Roman tradition in Arendt's analysis, the narrative persona takes up a position in discourse and assumes her rights as a legal subject. This positioning does not essentialise her either; it rather creates a person with whom one can be in dialogue, but also to whom one is responsible: 'a right-and duty bearing person, created by the law and which appears before the law', as Arendt has pithily remarked.[37] In the discussion of this paper, Désirée thus becomes a persona created by her narratives, but to whom I am accountable having taken up the responsibility of presenting her story as an Arendtian design that has a meaning; the latter is open to interpretation and negotiation between you as readers, myself as an author and narrative researcher and my narrative persona, whose stories should be open to all.

Fonds

During my archival research with Désirée's personal and political writings, the question of openness has particularly preoccupied me for different reasons and from different perspectives. To start with I was deeply upset to find out that although she was a notable figure in feminist labour history, her papers were never collected and archived and organised as *fonds*. This notion originated in France in 1841, when archivists were asked 'to unite all the deeds which come from a body, an establishment, a family, or an individual'.[38] In this light, *fonds* were conceptualised as assemblages that were much more than a simple collection of papers; they included both substantial and contextual documents and charted authorial and discursive relations between private and public documents and the historical figures that had either originated them or featured in them. Seen from a Foucauldian critical perspective then, *fonds* flesh out the way documents connect within a collection, but they also expose hierarchical orderings, as well as power-knowledge relations at play. What I therefore suggest is that *fonds* create 'the order of the archive', which is how Désirée, alongside her other comrades, were excluded from their creation. Her letters and other articles are instead in the *fonds* of Saint-Simonian and Fourierist leaders Père Enfantin and Victor Considerant.

In thus addressing the question of openness, my first move was to create virtual *fonds* for Désirée Véret-Gay by bringing together existing biographical and autobiographical documents, archival sources, as well as publications from her and about her.[39] What first emerged from this reassembling was the interesting phenomenon of what I have called 'the name wars', quite simply Désirée's decision to reject her patronymic name and choose her own name, Jeanne-Désirée, to sign her letters and articles.[40] This is how my *narrative persona* explained her decision:

> Men give birth to doctrines and systems and baptise them in their name; but we give birth to people; we should give them our own name and take only the name of our mothers and of God. This is the law dictated to us by nature and if we continue to take the names of men and of doctrines we will be slaves.[41]

Beyond the first move of creating Désirée's virtual *fonds* and engaging with the symbolic pluralism of her different names, my approach to reading and understanding her narratives emerged from an overall feeling that Niamh Moore, Andrea Salter, Liz Stanley and Maria Tamboukou have called *archival sensibility*.[42] *Archival sensibility* encompasses a set of practices that highlight the need to study archival documents carefully, in the sense that they should not be simply treated as sources of nice quotations or as illustrations of an analysis that was not led by their study. Although we always go to the archive with some questions in mind, we should also let the narratives emerging from its documents surprise us, allow them to interrogate our a-priori judgements, understandings and prejudices and let them redirect our analytical paths and routes of interpretation. Archival documents will always offer us exciting stories or quotations but their place should be formative and not illustrative or simply evidentiary in our narrative analytics.

But there is more to *archival sensibility*: although archival documents are often assemblages of fragmented, broken and discontinuous narratives, traces of the past rather than representations or mirrors of it, their fragmentation is not to be continued in the researchers' discourse. On the contrary, we need to be sensitive to the lives of the documents found in the archive, try to understand and map the conditions of their possibility and attempt to imagine their lives before and after our encounter with them. Finally, we need to be sensitive to their potentiality, the forces and effects of their intensity, which we need to facilitate and set in motion, rather than block, hide or sidestep. Simply put, we cannot engage with documents of life while ignoring the life of documents within the archive and beyond.

I have been apprehensive of the danger of my narrative analytics stripping out the intensity of the stories that I have excavated in the archive of Désirée's papers. While trying to listen to some of the flickering stories that erupt from her documents, I have also allowed their order of discourse to mingle with my own interpretations and understanding. To do this I have created a virtual archival site, where apart from her *fonds*, I have carefully mapped the archival sources of my research, and wherever possible I have given links to the cited documents.[43] In offering my readers the opportunity to study and appreciate the documents' poetics, textual economy and discursive order, I have attempted to open up a dialogical scene wherein the inevitable dryness of the researcher's analysis can be livened up in its entanglement with the stories of its *narrative persona*; it is to some glimpses into these stories that I now turn.

Action and narration: in struggle and in love

> When in the last women's session, I said that I do not want the Saint-Simonian name it is not at all because I deny the good that Saint-Simonians have done, neither do I doubt the good that they will do. [...] If I wanted to place myself under a name it would be certainly theirs that I would take.

> But I feel that there is different *work to be done*. For me all social questions depend on women's liberation; she will resolve them all. It is therefore towards this aim that all my efforts tend. It is under the banner of the new women that I will relate everything I am doing for our emancipation. Women's cause is universal and it is no way only Saint-Simonian.[44]

With this article written on 4 November 1832 in the seventh issue of *La Femme Nouvelle*, Désirée publicly distanced herself from the Saint-Simonian movement she had so passionately embraced only two years earlier. It was the last article she wrote for the newspaper she had founded in August 1832. Among the many themes that have struck me when reading it, I was particularly impressed by the importance of the role of work in the first autonomous feminist movement. Indeed, what my overall analysis has shown is that 'the right to work' preceded 'the right to vote' in the histories of western feminism. Désirée's article in the first issue of the feminist newspaper outlines the importance of work in no uncertain terms:

> Young daughters of the people without any other knowledge than our religion and without any other resources than those produced with our needlework, we have begun a work, still small and obscure, but which will rapidly expand and will raise high political questions.[45]

In making this statement Désirée was aware of the material restrictions that her needlework imposed on the time and resources she could use for her political work, but she was also in the mood for leaping into radical futures. The notion of the importance of initiation, of making a new beginning was repeatedly flagged up in her articles, but it was mostly fleshed out in her decision to start a newspaper, the first to be written by [mostly] proletarian women only. As one of her co-editors, Suzanne Voilquin pithily put it in the last issue of *La Tribune des Femmes* in April 1834, Jeanne-Désirée 'was not the first to think of creating a women's newspaper, but was certainly the first to have the courage to do it'.[46]

Désirée was indeed courageous enough not only to initiate a feminist newspaper, but also to break her bonds with the Saint-Simonian movement when she realised that their doctrines and hierarchies had eventually excluded women, as we have already seen. But apart from being a feisty proletarian feminist, she was also a woman in love with the leader of the movement she was withdrawing from. Before breaking the ties with the Saint-Simonian circles, she sent a letter to Enfantin explaining the reasons for her detachment: 'I am of the people, as I always communicate with them when I see them gather in public squares'[47] she wrote. But despite her love for the people, which was immense and made her eyes 'fill with tears',[48] she could also understand that not all Saint-Simonian men were embracing the idea of women's equal participation in the movement. It thus fell on women to organise for a better future: 'for us women, our work starts, to us women the duty to search for social love'[49] Désirée was adamant that women should look elsewhere, that they should stop following men, since what they had to say was 'so different from the nature of men'.[50] In writing to Enfantin about the need for women's autonomous organisation, she was open and frank about the emotional difficulties of this decision. And yet her letter to the Saint-Simonian leader was a definitive adieu:

> It is something stronger than my will that makes me write to you [...] yet you are the only one with whom I can be free [...] I am strong enough to endure your frankness and your advice and I am not afraid any more of the influence that can interfere with my work [...] Farewell, I embrace you and all humanity![51]

But while celebrating the importance of work as a creative force of life and political action, Désirée was also critical of the drudgeries of industrial labour. Her letters to Charles Fourier from Manchester Square in London paint a grim image of a proletarian women's life in the early phases of the industrial revolution:

> The work is so unappealing that I would prefer to be in the galleys. We must work from seven in the morning until midnight at the earliest; you see there are only very short breaks during the day, so we don't really have time to eat

and we are subjected to the varying caprices of the stock market; oh what a stupid business is this, this civilised industry![52]

Not only was the young seamstress disillusioned and frustrated by capitalist exploitation, she had also come to interrogate some of Fourier's ideas about the power of love:

> You expect, my dear M. Fourier, that love will come along to distract me, the love of an Englishman, isn't this what you are thinking? In this they are the same as they are in mechanics. They can only handle the material side or a fanciful love that exists only in the imagination. I have had lovers here, I can confide this to you, but they have only given me sensual pleasures. The English are cold, egotistical, even in their pleasures, in making love, in dining. Everyone thinks only of himself. Never shall I have the sort of love I properly need. I have made my decision about it and have settled for pleasure.[53]

Désirée's sincere and lively letter to Fourier forcefully throws us into a material and grounded understanding of the affective forces that traversed the constitution of the *narrative persona*, as already discussed above. It was love as *Eros*, passion and desire, a force for life, a mutual recognition, a movement towards the other that Désirée was missing. In downplaying pleasure in the *narrative persona*'s epistolary discourse I do not want to imply, let alone suggest that Désirée did not experience pleasure in her life: her letter above is a testament to the opposite. But what also emerges from her discourse around desire, love and pleasure is that pleasure was for her a notion heavily invested and indeed constrained by the segmentarities of capitalism and patriarchy. It was only by following forces of passion and desire that she could envision a radical future. Her letters to Fourier thus opened up different spaces in the misery of her life in England and powerfully show that it was despite and not because of pleasure that she went on working, writing fighting and dreaming:

> My dear Mr. Fourier, if you were not a great genius, I would never dare write such silly things to you. I leave my pen roam free, certain that nothing can be lost with you and that, amid the complaints of this poor civilised creature, you will find a few seeds that will create a happy harmony between the pivot of my thoughts and your theory. This will be the only thing that will draw me out of my apathy and I always think about it in happiness; but a dry theory is only good for the spirit, I am therefore impatient to grow old, so that I can see the dawn of its materialisation.[54]

Désirée did indeed grow old to see the dawn of a different world for workers, but not so much for women. Writing to Considerant from Brussels she remembered Fourier's love as reciprocal recognition, as well as the soothing impact that their correspondence had upon her life as a struggling young seamstress, who was still dreaming of happiness:

> On the occasion of every anniversary of those who have gone, I need to remember them, be reflective. Fourier was the console of pains; for me as for the others

he loved. My youth, my social enthusiasm, my inexperience of life, inspired him to put reasoning into theory and track the reason of my sadness. 'You have so many dominant passions', he wrote to me and would urge me to believe in civilisations.[55]

Throughout her life, Désirée let her passions dominate her, perhaps this is why she kept her revolutionary spirit high even when she got married and had two children. 'We cannot die without finishing the work that has been at the heart of our whole existence'[56] she wrote to Enfantin on 8 February 1848, shortly before she joined the demonstrations and street fighting. The February revolution[57] initiated processes for the creation of a new body politic and it was in the revolutionary spirit of the days that Désirée took to the streets again, demanding that women workers should be part of the struggle for democracy; in linking the right to work with the right to vote she worked simultaneously for both:

> Citizens,
>
> Many isolated women are in a desperate situation, you will not want them to continue to be exposed to poverty or disorder. Good morals are the strength of the republics, and it is women who make the morals; the nation should honour women's work through your voice! With your will they should take part in the reorganisation that occurs; and you should encourage the principle of association for the work they do within their control.[58]

In gendering the February revolution's right to work, Désirée highlighted the necessity for women's work to be recognised and honoured. She particularly emphasised the fact that many women workers were isolated and indeed marginalised and erased within the deplorable conditions of home based work. As a counter action to isolation Désirée would flag up the principle of association retrieving it from the theoretical baggage of the romantic socialist movements of her youth. Her correspondence with Enfantin between January and April 1848 shows that it was not just memories that moved her actions: her present was fused with the ideas of her political actions in the past, enriched by the experiences of a fully active life.[59] In doing so she wrote against two real and discursive separations: the social and the political, as well as the private and the public. She was determined that a reorganisation of the public sphere of work was dependent upon a reorganisation of the private sphere of the family and that the two could not be separated: 'we urgently need to create national restaurants, as well as laundries and lingeries, where people can find cheap healthy food and orderly and clean care, which cannot be created in isolation and which women reunited in association can easily organise',[60] she argued.

During the time of the February revolution, Désirée wrote fiery articles in *La Voix des Femmes* first and then in *La Politique des Femmes*. What she mostly highlighted in her articles was the fact that although women's political aim was the same with men's, their perspective was different and thus 'we must each have our originality', so that 'under the vast banner of socialism women's politics can march in front alongside men's politics'.[61] *La Politique des Femmes* did not publish more than 2 issues as the very possibility of being involved in politics was denied to women by law in the summer of 1848. Désirée followed Deroin in editing *L'Opinion des Femmes*, but the continuing persecutions and political failures eventually took their toll on her enthusiasm and commitment. At the end of 1849, she had retreated from public life and she was eventually forced to take the route of voluntary exile in 1864, following her husband Jules Gay who had lost his permit to publish in France. In one of her last letters to Considerant she wrote about her life in dark times:

> I didn't use to like either Belgium, or the Belgians. I moved here against my will [...] And, well, now that I am as free as I have never been, I live here voluntarily and I feel more and more attached to them, having learnt to know them.[62]

Having written profoundly and tenderly about her life in exile, Désirée gave away the mystery of her passionate involvement and also of her recurrent disappearances from the editorial and activists' groups as well as the workers' associations she had so tirelessly work to put together: 'After the struggle I used to fly off into the clouds of reverie, where I fashioned an ideal world for myself. Real, earthly life has always been painful for me',[63] she wrote to Considerant in July 1891, shortly before she died. But what does it mean to escape 'the real'? It is on some reflections on how the figure of the *narrative persona* contributes to new modes of making sense of the subject that I now want to conclude this article.

Narratives of 'the real'

Post-structuralist approaches to the subject in feminist theory and beyond have acknowledged and indeed celebrated multiplicity, fragmentation, non-fixity and nomadism, but they have avoided or side-stepped the effects of 'the real', simply put the material components that are entangled in the discursive constitution of subjectivities. In this context, Katerina Kolozova has pointed to 'the need in twenty-first century continental philosophy to traverse the postmodern or poststructuralist limits of thought'.[64] Kolozova's take of 'the real' follows trails of Francois Laruelle's notion of *le vécu*,[65] the real as lived experience and not as the impossibility of its psychoanalytic take, mostly recognised in Judith Butler's influential theorisation of subjectivity.[66] 'The real does not take the form of the meaning that is ascribed to it',[67] Kolozova notes, since 'as soon as it becomes a meaning, it retreats as the real.'[68] It is precisely at this point that the configuration of the *narrative persona* has made a contribution. Although 'the real' fades away at the moment of its discursive inscription, it nevertheless leaves its traces in the stories that have revolved around *le vécu*. We have thus seen instances of 'the real' flickering in the epistolary narratives that Désirée wrote at the end of her life. What has also emerged from these narratives is a remembered unity of the self, a design of a life that has a meaning. It is the possibility of having a unity, albeit only in narrative terms, that the move beyond the post-structuralist denial or rejection of it allows for, through the configuration of the *narrative persona*.

Désirée emerges as a *narrative persona* through her memory journeys that she passionately retraced in her last letters to a comrade and lover of her youth. Her very first letter to Considerant in May 1890 vividly inscribes her will, but also her ambivalence and hesitation in drawing a pen-portrait of herself through triggering the memory of her addressee:

> Does Victor Considerant remember Jeanne-Désirée? If yes, he should write her a word. She has forgotten nothing, neither Fourier, nor the feelings of the 1832 youth, and in her voluntary solitude, she lives calm and her heart is filled with memories of all her passionate life.[69]

In using the third-person mode of address, Désirée created a space of both intimacy and distance in her epistolary relationship; she would never use it again in the rest of their correspondence that marks the last year of her life. Love moves Désirée's memory journeys in her letters to Considerant, but although it is related to *le vécu*, the lived experiences of her amorous relationship to one of the leaders of the Fourierist movement it is not dependent on it. It is rather conceived in unilateral terms, love as 'radical solitude' in Kolozova's theorisation.[70]

Désirée's sense of continuity at the end of her life that can only be traced in her epistolary narratives does not create an essence of the self, but it does mark a 'stance';[71] it becomes the vector of her *conatus*, the Spinozist force to go on living. 'There is an instance of continuity of the 'I' provided by the incessant effort of the body to preserve itself against the disintegration brought about and upon it by the subject', Kolozova has argued.[72] It is this 'I' that persists through the material continuity of its body and its lived experiences that emerges as the *narrative persona* of my understanding and analysis. Although I will never find 'the truth' about who Désirée 'really was', I have taken responsibility vis-à-vis 'the real' of her lived experiences, which I have traced, reassembled, reread and effectively rewritten, creating a form for her *narrative persona* to take a position in the archives of feminist history.

Notes

1. Désirée Véret, veuve Gay to Victor Considerant, letter dated 21 June 1890. Archives Nationales Archives Nationales de France, Fonds Fourier et Considérant, Correspondance des membres, Dossier 8, Lettres de Désirée Véret, veuve Gay (AnF/10AS42/8/DVG/59/2).

2. Victor Considerant (1808–1893) was a follower of Charles Fourier's ideas and a significant historical figure in the movement of French Romantic Socialism. See Jonathan Beecher, *Victor Considerant and the Rise and Fall of French Romantic Socialism* (Berkeley: University of California Press, 2001) for a rich intellectual biography.
3. Beecher, *Victor Considerant*, p. 441.
4. As I will discuss, Désirée used a range of different names to sign her personal and public writings. For the sake of clarity, I have thus chosen to use her first name only, although I return to the issue of names in the history of feminism, later on in the paper.
5. See Maria Tamboukou, *Sewing, Fighting and Writing: Radical Practices in Work, Politics and Culture* (London: Rowman and Littlefield, 2015) for an overview of this literature.
6. Désirée to Enfantin, letter dated 11 September 1831, p. 1. Bibliothèque de l'Arsenal, Fonds Enfantin, Ms7608/Correspondance du Globe (Dames)/Désirée (J.)/4 lettres/40(1) [in microform] (BnF/BdA/FE/Ms7608/CdG(D)/DJ/40,1).
7. There is a rich body of literature around Saint-Simonianism, see Pamela Pilbeam, *Saint-Simonians in Nineteenth Century France: From Free Love to Algeria* (Basingstoke: Palgrave, 2014) for an updated overview of this literature.
8. 'From my work you will know my name', *Apostolat des Femmes-La Femme Nouvelle*, 1.7 (4 November 1832), pp. 69–70. As I have discussed elsewhere in detail, this newspaper, which was initially named *La Femme Libre*, changed many names during the two years of its publication and I have tried to keep the historicity of these name changes in the citation. See Tamboukou, *Sewing, Fighting and Writing*.
9. Désirée to Charles Fourier, letter dated 14 August 1833, transcribed and published by Michèle Riot-Sarcey, 'Lettres de Charles Fourier et de Désirée Véret: une correspondence inédite', *Cahiers Charles Fourier*, 6.3–14 (1995), p. 6.
10. Anna Wheeler (1780–1848) was a political writer and passionate supporter of women's rights. She was a friend of the French Socialists and often travelled and worked in France. For more details about Wheeler's life and work, see Karen Offen, *European Feminisms 1700–1795: A Political History* (Stanford, CA: Stanford University Press, 2000).
11. Désirée to Considerant, letter dated 7 September 1890 (AnF/10AS42/8/DVG/62/2).
12. Désirée to Considerant, letter dated 2 October 1890 (AnF/10AS42/8/DVG/64/2).
13. For Owen's educational ideas, see Ian Donnachie, *Robert Owen, Owen of New Lanark and New Harmony* (East Linton: Tuckwell Press, 2000).
14. There is a rich body of historical studies around the February 1848 revolution, which initiated the Second Republic in the French political history. De Tocquevilles' *Recollections* is considered to be the classic source. See Alexis De Tocqueville, *Recollections: The French Revolution of 1848*, ed. J.P. Mayer and A.P. Kerr, trans. George Lawrence (New Brunswick: Transaction Publishers, 2009 [1969]).
15. See letterhead of Désirée's letter to Enfantin, dated 28 May 1856: '*Exposition Universelle 1855, Mention Honorable, Mme Gay, Modes, Rue de La Paix 19*', Bibliothèque Nationale de France (BnF), Bibliothèque de l'Arsenal (BdA), Fonds Enfantin ou Fonds Saint-Simonien, Ms7608/Correspondance du Globe (Dames)/Désirée (J.)/4 lettres/40-43 [in microform] (BNF/BdA/FE/CD/7728/163).

16. Désirée to Considerant, letter dated 17 September 1890 (AnF/10AS42/8/DVG/63/2).
17. Désirée Gay, *Éducation rationnelle de la première enfance: manuel à l'usage des jeunes meres* (Paris: Adrien Delahaye Librairie and Geneva: J. Gay et Fils, 1868).
18. Désirée to Victor Considerant, letter dated 3 October 1890 (AnF/10AS42/8/DVG/64/3).
19. Désirée to Considerant, letter dated 21 June 1890 (AnF/10AS42/8/DVG/59/2).
20. See Tamboukou, *Sewing, Fighting and Writing*.
21. Gilles Deleuze and Felix Guattari, *What Is Philosophy?* trans. Graham Burchell and Hugh Tomlinson (London, New York: Verso, 2004).
22. Deleuze and Guattari, *What Is Philosophy?* p. 62.
23. Ibid., p. 64.
24. Ibid.
25. Ibid., p. 65.
26. Ibid., p. 177.
27. Ibid., p. 65.
28. Jeanne-Désirée to Enfantin, letter dated 31 August 1932. BnF/BdA/FE/Ms7608/CdG(D)/DJ/42, 1–3. Also, in Riot-Sarcey, Michèle, *De la liberté des femmes: 'Lettres de Dames' au Globe (1831–1832)* (Paris: côté-femmes editions, 1992), pp. 74–7.
29. For a more extended discussion of narratives as force, see Tamboukou, 'Narratives as Force', in Mona Livholts and Maria Tamboukou (eds), *Discourse and Narrative Methods* (London: Sage, 2015), pp. 93–103.
30. Susan S. Lanser, 'Towards a Feminist Narratology', *Narrative Poetics*, 20.3 (1986), pp. 341–63 (p. 344).
31. Hannah Arendt, *On Revolution* (London: Penguin, 1990), p. 106.
32. Hannah Arendt, *The Human Condition* (Chicago: University of Chicago Press, 1998 [1958]), p. 8.
33. Adriana Cavarero, 'Politicizing Theory', *Political Theory*, 30.4 (2002), pp. 506–32 (p. 528).
34. Rosi Braidotti, 'Lines of Flight+Suicide', in Adrian Parr (ed.), *The Deleuze Dictionary* (Edinburgh: Edinburgh University Press), pp. 148–50 (148–9).
35. Arendt, *The Human Condition*, p. 10.
36. Ibid., p. 11.
37. Arendt, *On Revolution*, p. 107.
38. Sharon Thibodeau, 'Review of *The Archival Fonds: From Theory to Practice*', in Terence Eastwood (ed.), *Archivaria*, 36 (1993), pp. 256–8 (p. 256).
39. See https://sites.google.com/site/mariatamboukou/the-book-archive/virtual-fonds/desiree-veret-gay [Date accessed: 10 December 2017].
40. This was a collective decision that all the editors and the majority of the contributors of the first feminist newspaper followed. See Tamboukou, *Sewing, Fighting and Writing*.
41. *Apostolat des Femmes-La Femme Nouvelle*, 1.7 (1832), p. 70.
42. Niamh Moore, Andrea Salter, Liz Stanley, and Maria Tamboukou, *The Archive Project: Archival Research in the Social Sciences* (London: Routledge, 2016).
43. See https://sites.google.com/site/mariatamboukou/the-book-archive/archival-worlds [Date accessed: 10 December 2017].
44. *Apostolat des Femmes-La Femme Nouvelle*, 1.7 (1832), p. 69 (my emphasis).
45. *Apostolat des Femmes-La Femme Nouvelle*, 1.5 (1832), p. 36.
46. *Tribune des Femmes*, 11.2 (1834), p. 181.

47. Désirée to Enfantin, letter dated 20 October 1832, BnF/BdA/FE/Ms7608/CdG (D)/DJ/43, p. 1.
48. D to Enfantin, 20 October 1832, p. 1.
49. J-D to Enfantin, 20 October 1832, p. 2.
50. Désirée to Enfantin, 20 October 1832, p. 3.
51. Désirée to Enfantin, 20 October 1832, pp. 3–4.
52. Désirée to Charles Fourier, undated letter, written from 37 Duke Street, Manchester Square in London, cited in Riot-Sarcey, 'Lettres de Charles Fourier et de Désirée Véret', p. 6.
53. Riot-Sarcey, 'Lettres de Charles Fourier et de Désirée Véret', p. 7.
54. Ibid., p. 8.
55. Désirée to Considerant, letter dated 9 October 1890 (AnF/10AS42/8/DVG/66/1).
56. Désirée to Enfantin, letter dated 8 February 1848 (BnF/BdA/FE/CD).
57. There is a rich body of historical studies around the February 1848 revolution with de Tocquevilles' *Recollections* (2009) being the classic source. See also Jones, Peter, *The 1848 Revolutions* (New York: Routledge, 1991), 2nd edition for the wider context of the 1848 European revolutions.
58. Petition addressed by Désirée Gay to Louis Blanc on 2 March 1848; reprinted in *La Voix des Femmes*, 2.2 (1848).
59. There are 14 extant letters from Gay to Enfantin between 1846 and 1860 and 6 of them were written between January and April 1848: 1 January; 8, 25, and 26 February; 7 March and 4 April (BnF/BdA/FE/CD/7728/151-164).
60. Petition addressed by Désirée Gay to Louis Blanc on 2 March 1848; reprinted in *La Voix des Femmes*, 2.2 (1848).
61. Ibid.
62. Désirée to Considerant, letter dated 1 September 1890 (AnF/10AS42/8/DVG/61/1-3).
63. Désirée to Considerant, letter dated 6 July 1891 (AnF/10AS42/8/DVG/68/3).
64. Katerina Kolozova, *Cut of the Real, Subjectivity in Poststructuralist Philosophy* (New York: Columbia University Press, 2014), p. 1.
65. François Laruelle, *Introduction au non*-marxisme (Paris: Presses Universitaires de France, 2000).
66. See Judith Butler, *The Psychic Life of Power: Theories in Subjection* (Stanford: Stanford University Press, 1997).
67. Kolozova, *Cut of the Real*, p. 5.
68. Ibid.
69. Désirée to Considerant, letter dated 5 May 1890 (AnF/10AS42/8/DVG/57/1).
70. Kolozova, *Cut of the Real*, p. 11.
71. Ibid., p. 47.
72. Ibid., p. 48.

Disclosure statement

No potential conflict of interest was reported by the author.

'We fuck and friends don't fuck': BFFs, lesbian desire, and queer narratives

Sam McBean

ABSTRACT
The 'BFF' label is often used by mainstream media to closet what are actually lesbian relationships. Responses to the misuses of the label insist that friendship is an anachronistic code that erases same-sex desire in the present. This article considers whether a different approach is possible – whether friendship might not only erase lesbian desire but might enable queer narratives. It takes as its case study MTV's *Faking It* (2014–2016), a half-hour sitcom in which teenage BFFs, Amy and Karma, are misrecognised as lesbians. *Faking It* flips the misrecognition of lesbians as BFFs, having BFFs read as a lesbian couple. *Faking It* is a self-conscious show that understands itself as coming 'after' a degree of mainstreaming when it comes to LGBTQ representation on TV – Amy and Karma are celebrated by their peers and told they do not need to hide behind friendship. Yet, *Faking It* entwines friendship and queerness in productive ways, suggesting that the narrative of friendship might contain queer narrative possibilities. In dialogue with queer thinking on time and narrative, this article insists on reading the BFF narrative as overlapping with same-sex female desire in ways that are productive of, and enable, queer narrative.

The 'BFF' (Best Friends Forever) label has become a popular label for Hollywood same-sex female pairs. Magazines and online celebrity websites (and fans) obsess over who's BFF-ing with whom. Evidence is culled and presented from celebrity social media accounts (notably Instagram and Twitter), to produce narratives of growing fondness between female celebrities. Demonstrations of affection between celebrities are frequently re-posted, shared, blogged about, and discussed on all manner of media sites. It is noteworthy that in and around 2014 and 2015, the BFF label became controversial as many noted that mainstream news outlets were using it to describe relationships that fans either suspected were, or celebrities themselves confirmed as, sexual or romantic. For instance, the label was used to refer to pairs in which at least one is or was an 'out' lesbian/bisexual/queer individual – as in the cases of Michelle Rodriguez and Cara Delevingne, Alicia Cargile and Kristen Stewart, and Angel Haze and Ireland Baldwin. Indeed, as with Haze and Baldwin (to take one example), it frequently happened that these pairs were not BFFs but were definitely dating. In these high-profile instances, the BFF label seemed to hide or erase the possibility of same-sex desire. The BFF label is seemingly infantilising in its insistence on these relationships as adolescent – childish attachments that can only ever be temporary placeholders for future 'serious' heterosexual relationships. Following in the wake of the BFF's emergence has been criticism of what is seen as its erasure of same-sex female desire.[1] Haze, for one, during their relationship[2] with Baldwin, described the way that numerous media outlets referred to them as 'best friends, best friends for life, like we're just friends hanging out' leading them to insist: 'we fuck and friends don't fuck'.[3] This insistence on 'fucking' seems a necessary intervention into a BFF narrative that would seemingly negate same-sex female desire.

As I have suggested elsewhere,[4] this contemporary erasure might be usefully connected to a longer history that explores the textual invisibility of the lesbian – what Terry Castle names the 'spectral lesbian subject', a subject who haunts but remains invisible to patriarchal culture.[5] The insistence by contemporary media that same-sex female couples are BFFs produces the figure of the lesbian as again, an invisible or impossible subject in a heteronormative context. Moreover, it refuses the possibility of bisexual identity, or desire that does not seem to cohere clearly into an identity. It is notable, for instance, that many of the celebrities identified as BFFs resist identifying 'as' anything – Kristen Stewart, for one, continually refused to 'come out', stating that it did not resonate with her experiences.[6] If the misnaming of same-sex female relationships as friendships is currently 'epidemic',[7] as one website for queer women termed it in 2015, it also has a much longer history. As has been argued about the spectral lesbian subject, her very existence is constituted by her impossibility. In Valerie Rohy's words, 'rather than suppressing the idea of lesbian desire, the homophobic discourse of impossibility promotes and structures its articulation'.[8] Historically, as Rohy argues, it has been through the textual impossibility of lesbian desire, or a refusal of its existence, that lesbianism has come to be defined. Paradoxically then, lesbianism 'comes into existence through the agency of the definition that names it as nonexistent'.[9] Framed by this deeper history, the contemporary BFF narrative might be one way that same-sex female desire is not so much erased or silenced, but, conversely, expressed. The application of 'BFF' to any number of lesbian, bisexual, and queer relationships between women means that it is one way that these relationships become visible in the first place. The BFF narrative is one way that stories about lesbian desire, queer identity, and bisexuality circulate. To be clear, acknowledging the centrality of the BFF narrative to the reporting on contemporary same-sex desire is different to suggesting that it is not politically necessary to insist on lesbian or bisexual visibility. It is, however, to take seriously the BFF narrative's relationship to contemporary iterations of same-sex desire, focusing not on what it hides, but what it articulates.

Less concerned with narrating a history of lesbian identity and same-sex female friendship, this article takes as its focus a contemporary media moment in which the lesbian is not so spectral – a time in particular where lesbian, bisexual, trans, and queer women populate numerous television shows across numerous networks. Or, to follow Castle's language, a time where the lesbian is not just a haunting figure but a very material possibility – separated clearly, it seems, from same-sex friendship by Haze's iteration 'we fuck'. In this present, the code of friendship is received as both offensive and, for Eleanor Margolis writing for *The New Statesman*, anachronistic: 'throwbacks to a time when lesbians hid behind green doors and wrote a lot of sad poetry about one another'.[10] Friendship as a code for same-sex desire between women is expressed, in articles such as these, as out of synch with this present – a present where queer women do not have to hide behind the cover of narratives of friendship. As with Haze's iteration, there is a clear line between friends and lovers – fucking. There is no code necessary in a contemporary where women can insist that they are, indeed, fucking each other. Yet, perhaps there is reason to pull back on this present, to consider the so-called anachronistic, and to insist that friendship might not simply be an offensive erasure of lesbian or queer identity, but might instead be an ongoing site of queer narrative possibility in this present.

In this article, I argue for the queer narrative possibilities of female friendship through a case study of an MTV television show that emerged out of the same moment as the media obsession with same-sex female BFFs. The premise of *Faking It* (2016–2016) is that BFFs Amy (Rita Volk) and Karma (Katie Stevens) are mistakenly 'outed' by their classmates – their friendship is read as a lesbian relationship. Seemingly referencing the contemporaneous wave of the misnaming of lesbian couples as BFFs, the show asks instead what if same-sex female friendships were mislabeled as lesbian relationships? Rather than correct this misreading, Amy and Karma fake being lesbians to become popular, at what is described by another character, as their 'kumbaya, socialist freakshow of a high school'. If *Faking It* starts with a 'fake' story of lesbianism, it is not merely concerned with fake same-sex desire. One of the show's ongoing narrative tensions involves Amy's realisation at the end of the first episode that she has real feelings for Karma – that she might be a real lesbian. Indeed, their 'fake' kiss at the school assembly in the pilot episode inspires 'real' desire in Amy for Karma. *Faking It* thus suggests that the BFF narrative might in fact generate not just a 'fake' lesbian narrative, but a real one.

Faking It knowingly winks at a changed televisual landscape – if outing arguably, just under two decades ago, ended Ellen DeGeneres' *Ellen* (ABC, 1994–1998), lesbianism, on *Faking It*, is precisely what makes Amy and Karma cool. The show insists, in other words, that in the contemporary televisual landscape (and in life), there is no need for coded lesbianism or for the cover of friendship to represent the possibility of queerness – indeed, instead, there is good reason to think that the inclusion of LGBTQ characters is precisely what makes an MTV sitcom relevant (read: cool). *Faking It* is positioned as historically 'after' a degree of mainstreaming of LGBTQ characters on American television, a time, it seems, where the lesbian is not an impossible subject for TV. Yet, because the show self-consciously positions itself in a moment 'after' *Ellen*, it also equally self-consciously asks: what is a lesbian narrative? Is it still a televisual event? Can it fit in with the everyday flow of sitcom television? The show's self-conscious exploration of lesbianism as 'a story' makes it an exceptional case study for queer narrative theory. *Faking It* does not just tell a lesbian story or offer another site for the exploration of queer representation on TV. In having Amy and Karma 'fake' lesbianism, *Faking It* self-consciously explores the construction of a lesbian narrative. Moreover, in binding the lesbian story to a narrative of friendship, the show challenges a contemporary politics that refuses or resists friendship as only a 'cover' for lesbianism. Rather than view friendship as a cover for lesbianism, *Faking It* asks, can friendship be the cause of lesbianism? Persistently making narrative and time thematic concerns, this half-hour MTV sitcom provides a telling example of the ways that popular culture is a site ripe for queer time and narrative theorising. It also intervenes into a political moment that wants to move 'on' from same-sex friendship. *Faking It* challenges a contemporary politics that would move 'on' from friendship and insists instead that friendship might enable, rather than foreclose, queer narratives.

Queerness, television, and time

There now exists a substantial body of queer work that considers queerness a product of a relationship to temporality. This work, although described as a recent 'turn', might be said to have its roots in earlier work on sexuality and narrative.[11] Crudely, what this work might be said to share is an insistence that queer signifies or describes a resistance or inability to keep to heteronormative timelines. Jack Halberstam, for instance, argues that queers represent the possibility of temporalities that run opposed to heteronormative, reproductive time (governed by the incitement to marry and reproduce) – so that queer lives offer a 'break from heterosexual life narratives'.[12] Or, in Lee Edelman's *No Future*, queer is best figured as antagonistic to the temporality of political norms, which he names 'reproductive futurism'.[13] As Elizabeth

Freeman puts it, perhaps queerness is about 'inventing possibilities for moving through and with time, encountering pasts, speculating futures', in ways that are 'out of synch with state-sponsored narratives of belonging and becoming'.[14] While the connection is not always explicitly drawn, these arguments echo and build on earlier work by narrative theorists. Judith Roof, for instance, in *Come As You Are*, explores the reproductive temporalities of narrative, arguing for their relationship to heterosexuality.[15] Or, as D. A. Miller suggests, queer stories are those that resist closure and thus represent the 'discontents' of narrative.[16] Here, earlier explorations of narrative's reproductive temporalities produce queerness as bound to other kinds of time – antithetical to or unassimilable by narrative's heterotemporalities.

I start with the link between queer temporality theory and earlier narrative theory to draw attention to what I see as an ongoing suspicion in queer temporality work that queerness is not to be found within traditional narrative sites.[17] Suspicions about narrative's reproductive temporalities seem to continue to influence queer temporality work, which overwhelmingly focuses on experimental, and non-narrative forms.[18] In other words, in a very important way, queer temporality theory often works with the same archive as queer narrative work. As Susan S. Lanser notes, 'queer narrative theory reveals a disproportionate penchant for British modernists'[19] and similarly, queer temporality work is also marked by a focus on modernist literature.[20] Notably, popular media forms are almost entirely absent from both queer temporality and queer narrative theorisations.[21] There is particular silence around television. As Amy Villarejo puts it, queer temporality theory has remained strikingly quiet about 'the dominant system of temporal implantation of the past seventy years, that is, TV'.[22] To put it bluntly, television is not traditionally seen as the most experimental or queerest of mediums – notable here is Freeman's omission of television from her insistence that 'video, film, and installation' are the 'time arts'.[23] If film, video, or installation work might be explored as 'arts' for the queer temporalities they enable, then it seemingly follows that television is 'unartful'. As Gary Needham puts it, television's temporalities 'apparently chime with the rhythms of the everyday, reflecting the life schedules of its viewers in ways that assume an almost unchanging social and domestic organisation that is resolutely normative'.[24] In other words, the timing of television seems fundamentally unqueer, particularly if queerness is seen as aslant with or in opposition to what is normative. However, as Villajero argues, television and its consumption contains numerous temporalities, '[s]ynchronization, transmission, seriality, recursivity, pause and delay, rewind, repeat' that might 'organize, disrupt, or otherwise confront queer temporalities'.[25] Both Villarejo and Needham point to the potential for television to offer queerer temporalities than are usually presumed. In Needham's words, 'we should be looking at the temporal experience of television as a significant location of queerness: how meaning and non-heterosexuality is ordered and disordered, not merely through representation, but through time and its effects'.[26]

In turning then to an MTV programme, I want to open up the sites where we might read queer time and narrative, insisting that television's seemingly everyday and banal temporalities are an integral site to consider precisely because they have historically marginalised and denied queer narrative. Moreover, it is perhaps an even more pressing site to consider now as LGBTQ characters have seemingly become mainstreamed across numerous shows and networks. When we now do not need to look too hard to find numerous television stories featuring LGBTQ characters, what happens to the repeated insistence that queerness is antagonistic to narrative? Or that the lesbian is best understood as a textual impossibility? *Faking It* emerges then at a moment when it looks as though the everyday temporalities of television are newly becoming compatible with telling queer stories – its 'fake' lesbian premise can only exist because the 'story' of lesbianism (and particularly, coming out) is by now, apparently, so well known as to be a genre that can be 'faked'. In some ways, *Faking It* is an exceptional case study, a case study which makes 'the lesbian narrative' a self-conscious topic within the content of the show. Yet, it is also an entirely banal, entirely predictable, glossy MTV programme. I want to hold on to the exceptionality of *Faking It*, while also insisting on the possibilities for even the most banal, the most MTV, the most high school of programmes to be a site for locating an analysis of queer time and narrative.

Faking It aired on MTV for three seasons (2014–2016) as a serialised, half-hour comedy on basic cable television. The show's seriality was a defining aspect of its temporal structure. In its resistance to narrative closure, serialisation, according to Robyn Warhol, opens up a challenge to what is traditionally imagined as narrative's heterocentrism. As Warhol argues, given serialised fiction's 'structurally mandated impulse to defer ending indefinitely', the form tends 'to undermine the heterocentric marriage plot by unraveling instances of closure that turn out to be only provisional and temporary'.[27] Since a serialised show must never 'finish' – or in fact its narrative tension relies on not just the temporary, but the constant resistance to closure – the genre contains a structural resistance to narrative's heterocentric teleology. Or, in Warhol's words, serialised fiction 'has the potential to subvert dominant ideologies of sexuality'.[28] *Faking It* plays with this aspect of serialisation not only in terms of the marriage plot, but in terms of the 'settledness' of sexuality. Of course, in an important way, *Faking It* follows Karma as she uses the fake lesbian story and the popularity it brings her and Karma to get the attention of the so-called hottest boy in school, Liam Booker (Gregg Sulkin). Playing consciously with the titillation of lesbian sexuality, the show makes it clear that it is only when Karma is outed as a lesbian that Liam becomes interested in her. One reading of the show might suggest that it is yet another representation that focuses on heterosexual romance, with lesbianism as a side narrative, a temporary obstacle, or a titillating phase for Karma on her way to her heterosexual happy ending – forever deferred in serialised form.

However, I would instead insist that the show does more than focus on this marriage plot, offering instead a kind of queering of serialised form. Throughout the first two seasons of the show, tension is built not only around who will get together with whom (and the ensuing diversions that get in the way), but also, the gender of these pairings. For instance, *Faking It*'s first season has Amy and Liam both pursuing Karma. Depending on your reading of the situation, it is either Liam that gets in the way of Karma and Amy or Amy that gets in the way of Karma and Liam. While it is Amy who realises her feelings for Karma in the first episode, it is also Amy who sleeps with Liam at the end of the first season. So, while Liam pursues Karma in the first season (as does Amy), Amy and Liam getting together complicates the triangle's composition as being about Liam and Amy's mutual pursuit of Karma (as well as complicates Amy's sexual identity). Central to the show is the possibility that anyone might desire anyone else – indeed, it relies on the ongoing potential that Karma might also desire Amy. The love triangle in *Faking It* is thus complicated not only by deferred closure, but by the deferral of a settled sexuality. The play with the love triangle continues in the second season, where another love triangle emerges – this time it is the bisexual Wade who is the object of desire for both Karma and Shane. Through the mobilisation of the love triangle (made up of individuals with bisexual desires or unstable sexual identities), the show's seriality (and its need to keep delaying closure) is mobilised to queer effects. Not only is there ongoing tension around who will get (and stay) together, but *Faking It* also serialises desire as something unstable and sexual identity as open to constant deferral.

Faking It mobilises seriality to do queer work – using the deferral of closure not only to keep narrative tension around romantic coupling, but also to keep in tension multiple characters' sexualities. Yet, as a counterpoint to Warhol's arguments about the queer narrative possibilities of seriality, television (and the half-hour show) in particular has historically had a difficult time serialising homosexuality. Anna McCarthy points out that as sitcoms became serial, 'narrative development in sitcom was arguably a hetero privilege', 'where sitcom seriality seems to revolve around romance plots and couples'.[29] In other words, not only did serialised sitcoms tend to only develop straight characters (which gay or lesbian characters being featured in one-off episodes), the temporal demands of the everyday seemed to clash with the disruptive temporality of queerness. Using *Ellen*'s failure to remain on air after its protagonist, Ellen Morgan (Ellen DeGeneres) came out, McCarthy argues that in this case, while 'the network could support queer television as a spectacular media event, it could not sanction a lesbian invasion of serial television's more modest form of history making, the regularly scheduled weeks of televisual flow'.[30] She argues that the event of Ellen coming out could be incorporated into television's historicity; the show could not sustain itself as 'what we might call "uneventful" television'.[31]

Decades have passed since *Ellen* and in the intervening time many LGBTQ characters have appeared on American television, with ongoing serialised narratives.[32] Arguably though, *Faking It* remains notable as a half-hour comedy on basic cable that featured as one of its main protagonists a queer female character. Despite, or perhaps because of, the influx of LGBTQ characters on film and television, *Faking It* self-consciously engages with what kind of temporality queerness might have on television now. Notably, this can only occur because *Faking It* comes after the 'event' that was *Ellen*'s lesbian coming out. Indeed, in the second episode of the first season, Liam describes Amy and Karma as 'the school's Portia and Ellen'. Aligned with *Ellen*, and thus arguably one of the biggest events for lesbian visibility on American television, Amy and Karma's fake story becomes an instance to reflect on the historicity of lesbianism on television, or, *Faking It* reflects on what kind of event lesbianism might be now. Throughout the first season, it is their (presumed) sexuality that propels Amy and Karma into the spotlight at their high school. Amy and Karma become school celebrities the minute that they are outed as lesbians – they are repeatedly shown being interviewed by the school's media and posting images of themselves on social media. As Karma puts it, 'being gay finally made me interesting'. The management of their celebrity as Hester High's first out lesbians is an ongoing narrative concern – how they will represent themselves, manage their media personalities, and their relationship narrative. In the show's narrative, lesbianism, it is repeatedly insisted, is still an event. If Ellen DeGeneres' coming out was a historical moment on television, it was one that was risky and, arguably, had a negative outcome for the show itself. The contemporary, in *Faking It*, is different precisely because now the 'event' of Amy and Karma is celebrated. Yet, as *Faking It* suggests, the temporality of 'eventfulness' persists. On *Faking It*, Amy and Karma are singled out and made popular precisely because their coming out is still eventful. Or, the positive reception that they receive actually reinforces their lesbianism as eventful – notable in its 'firstness' at the school, even if they are not 'first' to come out on television, and indeed the fact that they come 'after' many other coming outs is precisely why they are celebrated.

Faking It, moreover, sees Amy worry about how long the eventfulness of their relationship can be sustained. Or, in other words, *Faking It* reflects on what kind of narrative temporality the lesbian plot might have if it is limited to the temporal structure of the event. Karma worries that her (fake) sexuality might be the most interesting thing about her and in this, she voices a fear not only about being a boring heterosexual, but also about the lesbian story's likely expiry date. How long can Karma sustain this story? How long can she stay interesting? Conversely, how long can *Faking It* sustain interest in a lesbian plot? Can a lesbian plot be something more than an event? How interesting can the couple remain on a day-to-day basis? Much as the narrative of their relationship is always already structured by its eventual collapse (the truth will come out; the act cannot continue indefinitely), the event of Amy and Karma seems to also have an expiry date. In other words, *Faking It* raises the ongoing potential difficulties of lesbianism on TV when it is structured by the temporality of eventfulness – the event always ruptures the everyday and is thus a difficult temporality to sustain across a serialised TV show. Yet, *Faking It* also offers a potential solution, a solution to counter the temporality of the event – the forever timing of the BFF narrative.

Faking It contrasts the historicity of Amy and Karma as Hester High's famous lesbian homecoming queens, with their long-lasting friendship. In other words, if lesbianism is an event of historical proportions, the show offers up the long-standing friendship narrative as having a different temporality. As I suggested in my introduction, the show might tell us something about how the BFF narrative enables an articulation of lesbian desire, even as it seems to make that desire impossible. It does this at the level of time and narrative – suggesting that the temporalities of friendship offer queer televisual narrative possibilities. Notably, it is their friendship that connects them to a deep history of television shows; they compare themselves, for instance, to Ethel and Lucy in *I Love Lucy* (CBS, 1951–1957). If the reference to Ellen Degeneres recalls the event of lesbianism on American television, Ethel and Lucy recall the long history of female friendship. Amy and Karma not only belong to a history of lesbianism on television (a recent and, perhaps, troubled one), they also, via their friendship, belong to a deeper historical time. On *Faking It*, it is this narrative of female friendship that is repeatedly represented as long-standing – as having both a connection to a longer television history, and a guaranteed futurity. If the show is keen to remind viewers about the celebrity status of Karma and Amy, it is equally insistent on the longevity of their friendship – its forever nature. Throughout the series, both characters repeatedly reflect on the longevity of their friendship, their shared history, and the imagined future they will have as best friends. If the lesbian narrative is spectacular, a media event, and a rupture to the everyday temporalities of Hester High, the show juxtaposes female friendship here as the mundane, the everyday, and the forever. The interest that the high school has in Amy and Karma's (fake) lesbian relationship is contrasted in the repeated boredom that characters express at their friendship – its inside jokes and shared past, a past uninteresting to anyone other than the two of them. If the lesbian narrative is a spectacle, the BFF narrative is longevity and banality.

Yet, if the two temporalities are seemingly contrasted, *Faking It* insists that the forever temporality of friendship is precisely what enables the lesbian narrative. The show is fundamentally about Karm and Amy's friendship – within which Amy's desires emerge. In season two, Karma and Amy attempt to reconnect after they fight at the end of season one. Karma uses the language of romantic love to convince Amy that they need to make up, explaining, 'We're spending the rest of our lives together so we have to work this out.' The very fact that the lesbian narrative is believable in the first place, or, the reason that Amy and Karma are mistakenly outed is precisely because the pair does not actually have to fake anything. As Amy insists in season one, episode five, '[w]e're not acting like lesbians, we're acting like best friends'. In some ways, the show's insistence that female friendship can look like a lesbian relationship might be troubling. Indeed, much like the misrecognition of same-sex couples as friends functions as an erasure of the specificities of homoeroticism, the show's continued insistence that Amy and Karma's friendship is 'like' a lesbian relationship might be said to de-sexualise lesbianism.[33] Of course, the conflation of (especially historical) female friendship with lesbianism has been much debated and has led Sharon Marcus to argue that 'we need distinctions that allow us to chart how different social bonds overlap without becoming identical'.[34] The concept of overlap is a productive one for exploring the links between lesbianism and friendship in *Faking It*. While the show reveals the 'lesbian-like' friendship of Amy and Karma, it does not suggest that all female friendships are lesbian-like and it is also careful to show that Amy is not satisfied with just friendship – indeed, the show does not so much eradicate the distinctions between lesbian desire and same-sex female friendship, but rather complicate its boundaries. *Faking It* mobilises female friendship not as a way of de-sexualising lesbian sexuality – indeed, Amy's relationship in season two with another woman is by no means devoid of sex – but instead, I am arguing, suggests that the temporalities of same-sex female friendship might be a way to enfold queerness into the everyday fabric of cable television. Contrasted with the historical event of their relationship is the everydayness of their friendship – yet, *Faking It* refuses to only contrast these two temporalities. In enfolding Amy's lesbian desire into friendship, the show does not so much de-sexualise or de-particularise same-sex female desire, so much as.suggest that the temporalities of friendship offer something to a televised queer narrative. *Faking It* both reflects upon the limitations of queerness' relationship to television's temporalities (when it appears as 'event'), while also uses the everyday BFF temporalities to tell a serialised lesbian narrative. Here, the BFF narrative produces the possibility of the lesbian one.

Belatedness, negativity, and friendship

Faking It, as I have been arguing, draws attention to and foregrounds questions of narrative – in particular, same-sex female desire and its narrative temporalities. Moreover, I have been suggesting that the show offers a case study for considering how contemporary BFF narratives might not so much obliterate same-sex female desire, but actually enable its articulation. In this final section I want to explore the way that *Faking It* defines Amy (its queer female lead) through her belated or late timing. In this, the show again explores queerness via temporality, and again, I will suggest, makes Amy's queer narrative dependent on or co-emergent with (rather than separate from) a narrative of same-sex female friendship. Amy, in the first season, is characterised by a kind of trailing behind – she fakes coming out only to realise she actually is a lesbian. She belatedly comes to realise that she is what she said she was. This positions her as always one step behind the narrative that is always ahead of her. She is already 'out and proud', so the promise of her 'real' lesbian identity being consolidated already exists in the present, just ahead of her. She lags and lingers in its wake. As a commentator on the lesbian website AfterEllen writes, 'Amy may be doing the journey a little backwards.'[35]

There are compelling reasons to think that there is something 'backward' about the temporality of queer. Backwardness has been written on to queer bodies across the twentieth century, so that, as Heather Love puts it, queers are 'understood as throwbacks to an earlier stage of human development or as children who refuse to grow up'[36]: as '[p]erverse, immature, sterile, and melancholic', queers 'recall the past'.[37] On the other hand, Love also points out that 'backwardness has been taken up as a key feature of queer culture', gesturing for instance to camp's obsession with outmoded popular culture, or defiant refusals to grow up, or even to queer attachments to lost objects.[38] At a narrative level, there is also something backward about queer etiology. If the reviewer for *AfterEllen* suggests Amy is doing things a little backward, Kathryn Bond Stockton points out that this kind of backward etiology is typical for lesbian and gay narratives, which seemingly necessitate the production of a queer childhood after-the-fact – a gay child is always a backward construction. In Stockton's words, 'I must *become* who I say I've been' (emphasis in original).[39] Or, as Rohy puts it, 'the coming-out story always proceeds retroactively, compelling the gay individual to claim a new identity that has been there all along'.[40] If Amy belatedly needs to become who she has already said she is, this is not counter to, but actually completely indicative of the way that coming out creates as much as it supposedly consolidates an identity. *Faking It*, rather than doing things a little backward, actually performs the always-backward etiology of queer identity.

Amy trails behind not just 'her' lesbian narrative but also the affective present of the show – the happy narrative of pride that defines Hester High. Again, echoing the show's own coming 'after' watershed moments of queer representation on television, Amy supposedly comes out into a welcoming environment (rather than the hostility associated with the past). Rather than narratives of bullying and violence, *Faking It*'s universe relegates a hostile reception to queerness as a distant memory, a relic from the past. As Shane puts it in one episode, bullying the gays 'reeks of the late '90s'. Of course, the representation of Hester High as 'past' narratives of violence has been a point of criticism, where the show might be accused of ignoring the uneven and patchy equality afforded to LGBTQ people in the United States, where ongoing gendered and sexual violence (at both the state and individual level) continues to occur (particularly to queers of colour).[41] Yet, in the contemporary of Hester High, there is no room for gay bashing or, for that matter, shame, as Shane frequently notes throughout the series. In Shane's insistence on pulling Amy and Karma out of the closet, he tells Amy, 'You're gay and it's ok, there's no shame. [...] I was you once, so terrified of rejection that it took me forever to come out, but once I did, fourth grade got so much better, trust me.' Just as gay bashing belongs in the past, so too does a gay identity marked by shame. As David M. Halperin and Valerie Traub put it, gay pride rests on '[l]iberation, legitimacy, dignity, acceptance, and assimilation, as well as the right to be different: the goals of gay pride require nothing less than the complete destigmatization of homosexuality'.[42] In the proud present of Hester High, shame is the affect that comes before queer identity – the precursor to pride. Shame and negativity, in this narrative, are throwbacks to an era that is over. To feel shame is thus to be out of time with the current moment of pride, it is to be nothing less than a drag on the present. It is notable then that the show goes to great lengths to describe Amy as the bearer of 'bad feeling'.

Amy's story pulls back on the celebratory fake narrative, insisting on the ongoing existence of bad feelings in the present. Amy's feelings challenge the singular, progressive narrative of Hester High (and the mainstreaming of LGBTQ characters on television), refusing narrative cohesiveness and instead pointing toward ongoing discontents. If there is something queer about this (and I am suggesting there is), it is played out again through friendship. Throughout the series, Amy tells the story of having fallen for her best friend Karma again and again. In season two, episode three, Amy repeats it to a Brazilian foreign exchange student with a sigh, 'I fell in love with my best friend and I finally got the guts to tell her and everything got weird.' In opposition to the fake lesbian narrative of pride and acceptance that has Amy moving out of the closet and into happiness, *Faking It* offers the circular and repetitive story of Amy's unrequited love for her best friend. As she tells this story to Shane, to her mother, and even on a date, Amy's story repeats and Amy refuses to move on. The repetition of Amy's story is then echoed in other queer female characters on the series. On her first date with a woman, Amy confesses, 'I kissed my best friend Karma and now nothing makes sense.' Commiserating, her date replies, 'Been there, sister', and proceeds to share her own story of falling in love with and then being rejected by her best friend. This narrative of rejection by another woman who is not a 'real' lesbian is again repeated by Amy's eventual girlfriend of season two, Reagan (Yvette Monreal). In Reagan's story her girlfriend goes back to her first boyfriend, explaining that Reagan was 'just a phase'. The repetition of the narrative of lesbian bad feeling jams the narrative of pride, demonstrating the excesses or discontents of this narrative.

Moreover, in these narratives of bad feeling, friendship or feelings for straight female friends are of primary importance. Characters' same-sex desires and queer feelings are, in many ways, stuck in friendship – originating there and also remaining attached to straight female friends in what is imagined as a backwards orientation. In the first episode when Amy describes Karma as her 'friend', Shane mocks her, suggesting that 'friend' is a euphemism, and an old, tired one at that. Here, Shane implicitly draws attention to 'friend' as a shameful cover for a queer relationship. Echoing Angel Haze's annoyance at having their relationship referred to via the label of 'BFFs', Shane seems to hail a contemporary moment in which lesbian desire does not have to 'hide' behind a narrative of friendship. While claiming a visibility for lesbian desire, it also says no to what is frequently imagined as a presumed 'older' form of lesbian identity (romantic friendship, closetedness). Of course though, Amy is not hiding behind the cover of friendship. As I have suggested, *Faking It* continuously gestures to the possibilities of the BFF narrative – and to what kinds of queer narratives it might offer.

In many ways, this article was driven by my desire not to reject the BFF narrative in favour of the lesbian one. I want to insist on the possibility for friendship as not only or necessarily producing a de-sexualised narrative of lesbianism or an erasure of lesbian desire in the present. As demonstrated in *Faking It*, friendship might conversely be the cause of queerness – where Amy's desire is awakened precisely because she fakes being a lesbian for her BFF. Rohy argues that etiology is a particular narrative concern for queerness – so that there is an obsession in homophobic and heteronormative culture with finding 'a narrative of causation, a theory of what makes people gay or lesbian'.[43] While predominant American gay and lesbian liberal rhetoric revolves around claims to being 'born gay', *Faking It* offers a queerer genealogy. Borrowing Rohy's term, the show flirts with the idea of 'homosexual reproduction' in its postulation that Amy's queer desires arise from a performance of lesbianism.[44] Rohy uses homosexual reproduction to refer on the one hand to the fears of cultural spread or influence that are attached to homosexuality, while also to reclaim a queer position that might offer an alternative to 'born gay' etiologies. Here, it is the narrative of queerness that multiplies to produce yet another narrative: the fake lesbian story births a real lesbian.

Or, from another angle, the BFF story births a lesbian one. In one trailer for the show, titled 'How far would you go?', MTV asks, 'What would you do … for your BFF?'. It asks 'Would you … knock someone out?' or 'Would you … break the law?', screening clips from other MTV shows which show friends doing just these things. The trailer insists that, 'Your BFF would do anything for you' and then asks, 'But would you … fake being a lesbian?' Offering teaser scenes from *Faking It*, the short clip finally proclaims, 'MTV Brings BFF to a whole new level!' In this trailer, the lesbian is not oppositional to a best friend – indeed, lesbianism is something that Amy does for her best friend. As Karma explains it in one episode, 'Don't think of it as lying, think of it as a gift to your oldest and dearest friend.' In some ways then, the origin of the lesbian story can be found in the best friend story. Here, it is the BFF narrative that ends up producing lesbian desire and queer feelings. *Faking It* also gestures to the possibility that Karma's feelings for Amy might similarly exceed the BFF narrative. Throughout the seasons, there is cause again and again to suspect that Karma might desire Amy in the same way that Amy desires Karma. If I began this essay by considering how the BFF label might represent a contemporary way that same-sex desire is articulated, here, *Faking It* offers a narrative of lesbianism and friendship that resists imagining friendship as erasing lesbian desire. In *Faking It*, lesbian desire emerges out of, is enabled by, and even potentially caused by the BFF narrative. *Faking It* pulls us back into the queer potentials of same-sex female friendship narratives, offering a way perhaps to consider the overlaps of friendship and desire – the queer narratives produced by same-sex female friendship.

Notes

1. See, for instance, Eleanor Margolis, 'No more "Gal Pals": Why Do We Assume Lesbians Are Confused, Attention-Seeking, or Man-Boycotting Straight Women?', *New Statesman*, 22 April 2015. http://www.newstatesman.com/lez-miserable/2015/04/no-more-gal-pals-why-do-we-assume-lesbians-are-confused-attention-seeking-or [Date accessed: 31 August 2015].
2. Subsequent to the press that Haze and Baldwin received, Haze has stopped publicly identifying as female and now uses the pronouns 'they/them'. In referring to Haze and Baldwin as women in a relationship, I use the language that Haze, and the media more widely, used in 2014 to describe their relationship.
3. Ella Alexander, 'Angel Haze interview: Lesbians, Marriage, Rap and Depression – Inside the Mind of Hip-Hop's Irrepressible Female Artist', *The Independent*, 27 June 2014. http://www.independent.co.uk/news/people/angel-haze-interview-lesbians-marriage-rap-and-depression--inside-the-mind-of-hiphops-irrepressible-female-artist-9566207.html [Date accessed: 31 August 2015].

4. Sam McBean, 'The "Gal Pal Epidemic"', *Celebrity Studies*, 7, no. 2 (2016), pp. 282–284.
5. Terry Castle, *The Apparitional Lesbian: Female Homosexuality and Modern Culture* (New York: Columbia University Press, 1993), p. 8.
6. Margaret Wappler, 'Riding Shotgun with Kristen Stewart', *Nylon Magazine*, 12 August 2015. https://www.nylon.com/articles/kristen-stewart-september-2015-cover [Date accessed: 31 August 2015]. Stewart has since come out as 'gay', on the television show Saturday Night Live in February 2017.
7. Carolyn Yates, 'Gal Pals in History: 8 Ways to Avoid Using the Words "Lesbian" or "Bisexual"', *Autostraddle*, 29 May 2015. http://www.autostraddle.com/gal-pals-in-history-8-ways-to-avoid-using-the-words-lesbian-or-bisexual-291513/ [Date accessed: 31 August 2015].
8. Valerie Rohy, *Impossible Women: Lesbian Figures & American Literature* (Ithaca, NY: Cornell University Press, 2000), p. 1.
9. Rohy, *Impossible Women*, p. 2.
10. Margolis, 'No more "gal pals"'.
11. Carolyn Dinshaw and others, 'Theorizing Queer Temporalities: A Roundtable Discussion', *GLQ: A Journal of Lesbian and Gay Studies*, 13.2-3 (2007), 177–195 (p. 177). For an earlier postulation on the figure of the lesbian as a temporal construction, see Annamarie Jagose's, *Inconsequence: Lesbian Representation and the Logic of Sexual Sequence* (Ithaca, NY: Cornell University Press, 2002).
12. Judith Halberstam, *The Queer Art of Failure* (Durham, NC: Duke University Press, 2011), p. 70.
13. Lee Edelman, *No Future: Queer Theory and the Death Drive* (Durham, NC: Duke University Press, 2004), p. 2.
14. Elizabeth Freeman, *Time Binds: Queer Temporalities, Queer Histories* (Durham, NC: Duke University Press, 2010), p. xv.
15. Judith Roof, *Come As You Are: Sexuality & Narrative* (New York: Columbia University Press, 1996).
16. D. A. Miller, *Narrative and Its Discontents: Problems of Closure in the Traditional Novel* (Princeton, NJ: Princeton University Press, 1989).
17. For a discussion of queer theory's emphasis on performativity over narrative, see Lynne Huffer, *Are the Lips a Grave?: A Queer Feminist on the Ethics of Sex* (New York: Columbia University Press, 2013), p. 56.
18. For queer temporality theory that works with experimental video art and performance, respectively, see Freeman, *Time Binds*; and José Esteban Muñoz, *Cruising Utopia: The Then and There of Queer Futurity* (New York: New York University Press, 2009).
19. Susan S. Lanser, 'Toward (a Queerer and) More (Feminist) Narragology', in Robyn Warhol and Susan S. Lanser (eds.), *Narrative Theory Unbound: Queer and Feminist Interventions* (Columbus: The Ohio State University Press, 2015), pp. 23–42 (p. 26).
20. See, for instance, Heather Love, *Feeling Backward: Loss and the Politics of Queer History* (Cambridge, MA: Harvard University Press, 2007); Christopher Nealon, *Foundlings: Lesbian and Gay Historical Emotion before Stonewall* (Durham, NC: Duke University Press, 2001).
21. As an exception, see Jack Halberstam, *The Queer Art of Failure* (Durham, NC: Duke University Press, 2011).
22. Amy Villarejo, *Ethereal Queer: Television, Historicity, Desire* (Durham, NC: Duke University Press, 2014), p. 18.

23. Freeman, p. xviii.
24. Gary Needham, 'Scheduling Normativity: Television, the Family, and Queerness', in Glyn Davis and Gary Needham (eds.), *Queer TV* (Abingdon: Routledge, 2009), pp. 143–158 (p. 143).
25. Villarejo, p. 19.
26. Ibid., p. 157.
27. Robyn Warhol, 'Queering the Marriage Plot: How Serial Form Works in Maupin's *Tales of the City*', in Brian Richardson (ed.), *Narrative Dynamics: Essays on Time, Plot, Closure, and Frames* (Columbus: The Ohio State University Press, 2002), pp. 229–248 (p. 232).
28. Warhol, p. 232.
29. Anna McCarthy, '*Ellen*: Making Queer Television History', *GLQ: A Journal of Lesbian and Gay Studies*, 7.4 (2001), pp. 593–620 (pp. 598–9).
30. Ibid., p. 597.
31. Ibid.
32. For analyses of these representations, see Kim Akass and Janet McCabe (eds.), *Reading the L Word: Outing Contemporary Television* (London: I.B. Tauris, 2006); Rebecca Beirne (ed.), *Televising Queer Women: A Reader* (New York: Palgrave Macmillan, 2008); Pamela Demory and Christopher Pullen (eds.), *Queer Love in Film and Television* (New York: Palgrave Macmillan, 2013).
33. For an extended discussion of the theoretical tensions around reading lesbianism as closely related to female friendship, see Sharon Marcus, *Between Women: Friendship, Desire, and Marriage in Victorian England* (Princeton, NJ: Princeton University Press, 2007), pp. 10–4.
34. Marcus, p. 30.
35. Elaine Atwell, '"Faking It" recap (1.2): Homocoming', *AfterEllen*, 30 April 2014. http://www.afterellen.com/tv/216426-faking-it-recap-1-2-homecoming-out [Date accessed: 31 August 2015].
36. Love, p. 6.
37. Ibid.
38. Ibid., p. 7.
39. Kathryn Bond Stockton, *The Queer Child, or Growing Sideways in the Twentieth Century* (Durham, NC: Duke University Press, 2009), p. 184.
40. Valerie Rohy, *Lost Causes: Narrative, Etiology, and Queer Theory* (Oxford: Oxford University Press, 2015), p. 99.
41. For an exploration of how the inclusion of certain forms of homosexuality in the national imaginary produces excluded others, see Jasbir Puar, *Terrorist Assemblages: Homonationalism in Queer Times* (Durham, NC: Duke University Press, 2007).
42. David M. Halperin and Valerie Traub, 'Beyond Gay Pride', in David M. Halperin and Valerie Traub (eds.), *Gay Shame* (Chicago, IL: The University of Chicago Press, 2009), pp. 3–40 (p. 3).
43. Rohy, *Lost Causes*, p. 2.
44. Ibid.

Disclosure statement

No potential conflict of interest was reported by the author.

A moving target – cognitive narratology and feminism

Karin Kukkonen

ABSTRACT
The present article develops a feminist approach to cognitive narratology on the basis of recent work in embodied cognition. Cognitive narratology does not traditionally consider gender perspectives, for a variety of reasons, none the least because the gendering of brains into 'male' and 'female' is deeply problematic. Contemporary cognitive narratology moves its point of interest however from the brain to the larger connections between brain, body and their situatedness in the world. From this new, embodied approach to cognition, we work toward a feminist dimension for cognitive narratology, drawing on issues of performativity, habitus and interpellation and highlighting the degree to which the notion of embodiment brings together both cognitive and cultural aspects of narrative. On the example of Hilary Mantel's short story 'The Assassination of Margaret Thatcher' (2014), we outline the complex ways in which narration, body images/body schemata, and metaphors interact and how these interactions can be analysed by an embodied feminist narratology that takes seriously both the embodied engagements of reading narrative and the edge within it that literature reveals.

When Terry Castle reviewed the collection *The Assassination of Margaret Thatcher* for the *New York Times* (2 October 2014), she stressed that author Hilary Mantel has 'assumed an esteemed place in what might be called a great tradition of modern British female storytelling', placing her next to a whole slew of names from Virginia Woolf to Zadie Smith. 'Second thought', she interrupts this seemingly obvious way of talking about Mantel. 'Despite having just done so, does one really want to organize artistic affinities by sex?' Arguably not; and she swiftly introduces a comparison with a male author before carrying on with her review of Mantel's short stories. Castle's move demonstrates the gendered logic in thinking about literary contexts and traditions of storytelling, especially when addressing a non-academic audience.

Despite having won the Booker Prize twice, Mantel still awaits discovery for literary criticism and narratology, so I can only speculate about how cognitive narratology at large would approach *The Assassination of Margaret Thatcher*.[1] It seems fair to assume, however, that an analysis from the point of view of cognitive narratology would not concern itself with 'a great tradition of modern British female storytelling', because categories of history ('modern'), politics ('British') and gender ('female') tend to be side-lined in favour of seemingly neutral notions such as narrators, focalisers (or fictional minds), prototypical story scripts, as well as fictional worlds. Cognitive narratology draws on research in the neurosciences, social cognition and discourse psychology in order to develop models of how readers understand the fictional narratives of literary texts. Readers might construct a mental model, also called a 'storyworld', in which characters can be related to each other in the course of a narrative and which can be compared to other possible worlds or mental models. Scripts of stories or real-world experience might be deployed to make sense of narratives, and the minds and intentions of characters can be accessed through the cognitive capacity of 'theory of mind' with which we gauge the thoughts of our real-world partners in conversation, too.[2] While cognitive narratology does not ignore the contributions of feminist narratology to the consideration of gender aspects in narrative perspective, emotional engagements of readers and gender-specific plot types, it rarely brings them into contact with mental models, story scripts and theory of mind, and makes no general statements on how cognitive and culturally embedded aspects of narrative, including gender, can be combined.[3] Cognitive narratology, like the traditional narratology that took science as its template, pulls away from historically embedded phenomena in favour of greater generality and abstraction.

While cognitive narratology would certainly not deny that narrative pertains to the situations men and women find themselves in, respectively, in cultures around the world, the links to cognitive processes (that interest cognitive psychology) and the build-up of the brain (that interests neuroscience) are difficult to ascertain, and gender becomes a moving target seemingly outside the reach of the cognitive approach. Most scientific studies in the cognitive sciences, conducted on male, white US college students, consider cognition in gender-neutral terms. And when gender differences are observed in the cognitive work that informs this strand of narratology, they very quickly lead to the notion of an essential and holistic difference between the 'male brain' and the 'female brain' that quaintly confirms established gender stereotypes. Simon Baron-Cohen's *The Essential Difference* is a striking example of how a cognitive capacity, which is a priori gender-neutral, namely, theory of mind, then turns into a distinguishing feature of the 'female brain', which is gendered as empathetic and sociable.[4] While Baron-Cohen's work on theory of mind has been taken up very successfully in cognitive narratology by Lisa Zunshine and others, these gender-related aspects have been largely ignored.[5] This is perhaps wise, since Baron-Cohen's notion of 'essential differences' and other cognitive and neuroscientific work assuming there is a demonstrable distinction between male and female brains are criticised by female scientists as lacking appropriate evidence and engaging in what they, fittingly, call 'neurosexism'.[6] If cognitive narratology were to subscribe to the view that the male and the female brain are essentially different, it would be very hard to avoid such 'neurosexism'. If cognitive narratology, on the other hand, assumes that the brains of men and women are basically alike, then it seems that the approach would have nothing to say on gender differences at all, because these would fall out of its remit of interest and inquiry.

'Feminist narrative theory has ... least in common with cognitive narratology,' writes Robyn Warhol in the volume *Narrative Theory*, where proponents of rhetorical, feminist, cognitive and unnatural narratology enter into debate.[7] In his response at the end of the volume, David Herman, who represents cognitive narratology, suggests that the embodied, 'post-Cartesian' approach to cognition could counter Warhol's argument that cognitive narratology's 'universalism ... overlooks the differences born of identity positions'.[8] Herman leaves it at this gesture, perhaps, because the scientists and philosophers in embodied cognition whom he cites also have not considered gender perspectives in their accounts.[9] It seems to me, however, that a related approach, the current perspectives on cognition as an embodied process of probability and prediction that connect easily to cultural modes of meaning-making (for short, the so-called predictive processing model), could indeed enter into a conversation with feminist narratology and feminist literary theory more generally. Predictive processing conceives of cognition across many layers as built on predictions and the way in which they are weighted with probabilities. When you reach for this special issue of *Textual Practice*, for example, the muscles in your hand already prepare the right grip before your fingers have even touched the cover; and, as you scan the text, your skills in reading English already allow you to predict the next couple of words through probable patterns of syntax and idioms. Embodied movement, perception, but also cultural skills like reading depend on a complex set of predictions about our environment, where surprises (or, prediction errors) lead to a revision of the predictive, probabilistic model of the world that underlies cognitive processes.[10] Gender, I am going to argue, needs to be fundamentally integrated into the connections between embodiment and predictions on which the approach relies. In turn, such an integration allows cognitive narratology a sustained perspective from which to address the moving target of gender.

1. Sheaths of embodiment

The title story of Hilary Mantel's collection, 'The Assassination of Margaret Thatcher', presents the prime minister's (historic) visit to an eye clinic in Windsor in the spring of 1983 through the narration of a resident of the town who unwittingly invites a man into her flat who intends to shoot Thatcher dead.[11] While the narrator and the assassin wait for Thatcher to emerge from the eye clinic, they share their views on Britain's first female prime minister. The narrator, whom readers are invited to picture as a middle-class intellectual with pretensions of open-mindedness, is eerily dispassionate about the fact that a man with a gun and murderous intentions sits in her flat or about the prospect that Thatcher is about to be shot from her living room window. The narrator and the assassin agree that Thatcher must die. It all ends with these lines from the female narrator:

> High heels on the mossy path. Tippy-tap. Toddle on. She's making efforts, but getting nowhere very fast. The bag on the arm, slung like a shield. The tailored suit just as I have foreseen, the pussy-cat bow, a long loop of pearls, and – a new touch – big goggle glasses. Shading her, no doubt, from the trials of the afternoon. Hand extended, she is moving along the line. Now that we are here at last, there is all the time in the world. The gunman kneels, easing into position. He sees what I see, the glittering helmet of hair. He sees it shine like a gold coin in a gutter, he sees it big as the full moon. On the sill the wasp hovers, suspends itself in still air. One easy wink of the world's blind eye: 'Rejoice,' he says. 'Fucking rejoice.' (p. 288)

The narrator adds mock-heroic touches to her description of the prime minister's attire. Her famous handbag is 'slung like a shield' and her signature 'do turns into a 'glittering helmet of hair'. In this context, even the 'tailored suit' resembles a suit of arms. In the mock-epics of the eighteenth century, the commodity culture of the modern age is ridiculed when placed against the ancient, epic model. The brocades, silks and carefully pressed locks in Alexander Pope's *The Rape of the Lock* (1714) present the battles over female honour fought in the eighteenth-century drawing room as encounters that gain ironic edge when juxtaposed with the conventions of the *Iliad* or *Aeneid*. Mantel's narrator considers Thatcher's insignia of power-dressing and her assumption of a male way of speaking similarly as 'ridiculous'. 'It's the fake femininity I can't stand, and the counterfeit voice' (p. 266). Thatcher, according to Mantel's narrator, 'can't see how ridiculous she is' (p. 274).

But Thatcher's power-dressing comes with real power. She does not have to rely on the poet Pope to inscribe her name '"midst the stars'. And ridiculous as it might sound when she said in an actual interview, 'Of course I am obstinate in defending our liberties and our laws. That is why I carry a very large handbag,'[12] the obstinacy that is captured by the handbag is real and merciless. The assassin understands this. 'It's not about her handbag. It's not about her hairdo' (p. 275). As becomes clear in the conversation between Mantel's narrator and the assassin, he does actually not 'see what I [the narrator] see'. His view of Thatcher and her body is very different, as emerges when he mentions the hunger strikes by Bobby Sands and others in Northern Ireland in 1981 in their bid to claim status as political prisoners from Thatcher's government. 'Your body digests itself. It eats itself in despair. You wonder why she can't laugh? I see nothing to laugh at' (p. 276). In both the assassin and the narrator, the hatred of Margaret Thatcher is connected to the body, but the modes of embodiment which are addressed are very different.

The narrator refers almost exclusively to the way in which Thatcher dresses, presents and comports herself, that is, her 'body image'. The assassin, in contradistinction, seems to focus on the way in which her body is experienced pre-consciously, that is, the 'body schema' of Thatcher (and her victims). Body image and body schema refer to the ways in which embodiment connects to the cultural manipulations of movement, dress and looks and to the pre-conscious processes of muscles, neurons and brain chemistry respectively.[13] Mantel draws on both these modes of embodiment and plays them off against each other. While the narrator is not physically threatened by Thatcher, as a self-described member of the intelligentsia, she is culturally threatened by her. In one of the very few instances where Mantel's narrator breaks her mock detachment from Thatcher, we read the following: 'I thought, there's not a tear in her. Not for the mother in the rain at the bus stop, or the sailor burning in the sea. She sleeps four hours a night. She lives on the fumes of whisky and the iron in the blood of her prey' (p. 278). Underneath the surface of ridiculous power-dressing and protective 'dos, the narrator comes to understand, there is a predator. For a moment, the narrator moves away from the mock-heroic incongruence in the appearance of the prime minister and relates the assassin's perception of her as a visceral creature conceived in hyper-masculine terms. In this dialogue of embodied perspectives between the narrator and the assassin, Mantel develops a multi-layered image of sheaths of embodiment in 'The Assassination of Margaret Thatcher'.

Thatcher as predator implies a merciless creature that tears at its victims and thrives on their misery. Such an embodied literary image depends on the ingestion of the harsh substances of whisky and blood and the pre-conscious verbal senses of smell and taste which they refer to. Thatcher as a mock-heroic politician, in turn, implies a ridiculous posturing unaware of its own insufficiency. Thatcher's 'tottering' style of walking in high heels, her choice of clothing and the gestures of protection and attention which her handbag and hairdo imply make for a sharp contrast through a difference between body image and body schema connected to the perspectives of the narrator and the assassin. Both images capture the embodied nature of Thatcher, but Mantel chooses not to present the prime minister, who does not appear until the end of the short story, in terms of fixed embodiment. She captures imaginatively her way of relating to the environment and her impact on her contemporaries.

As the cognitive narratologist looks into the embodied dimension of cognition in Mantel's text, she draws out the verbs of motion with their particular embodied phenomenology (such as 'totter'), sensual perception (such as 'fumes of whisky') and descriptions of bodily constraints and freedoms (such as 'slung as a shield'). From these elements, an embodied image of the character and her relationship to the environment emerges that can sometimes be tied to a particular narrative perspective, such as the Mantel's narrator. The literary text conjures a richly inhabited lifeworld that is thick with embodied experiences.[14] If second-generation cognitive approaches to narrative are right, then these embodied uses of language create embodied resonances in readers which echo the 'tottering' of the mock-heroine and the perception of 'fumes' of the predator, leading readers to embody the two perspectives themselves. The predictive aspect sharpens the importance of such embodiment. One is likely to perceive different aspects as salient when Thatcher appears a mock-heroic politician than when she appears as a predator. A different repertoire of comportment and interaction emerges, a different way of judging these interactions (and hence forming new expectations), and eventually a different probable conclusion to the narrative plot. There is a clear connection, from such a perspective, between the bodily experience, one's thoughts or intentions about objects in the world and one's actions within that world. Mantel asks her readers to move through different layers of embodiment as her narrator and the assassin lay in wait for a glimpse of the prime minister. The two different modes of embodiment are not simply limited to the physical appearance of Thatcher. They also imply two different ways of interacting with others and affecting others' lives, and, in turn, they suggest different appropriate ways of responding to her. Within the plot of the fictional narrative, they also outline different ways for how the story is likely to end: the tottering mock-heroic politician could simply disappear into obscurity, while the predator needs to be put down.

Drawing on embodied cognition and predictive processing, I have elsewhere discussed these connections in terms of 'cascades of cognition', where the different levels feed into each other. Bodily experience and the expectations of how the physical and cultural environment responds to our actions enters a feedback loop that starts modifying each other, and that can be dramatised in the development of a literary scene or plot.[15] Because of the core role of probability and prediction, this strand of cognitive narratology allows us to think of the richly inhabited lifeworld as structured along gender-lines and the predictions around embodiment that can be coded as predominantly female, such as the mock-heroine, or predominantly male, such as the predator.

2. Performance, habitus and interpellation

In the framework of embodied predictive processing, cognitive narratology is not on neutral ground anymore. The necessity to discuss gender becomes even clearer, perhaps, once we turn our attention to the embodied practices that are traditionally confined to the cultural sphere but that should be considered, as I shall argue, as intimately entwined with processes of embodied cognition.

In the article 'Throwing Like a Girl', Iris Marion Young revisits Maurice Merleau-Ponty's phenomenological account of the 'lived body' from a gender perspective and draws attention to the pre-conscious ways in which girls and women constrain their own bodily movement in accordance with gender expectations. 'The space available to our movement is constricted space,' she writes.[16] In embodied cognition, the body's assessment of sensory-motor contingencies through which we relate to the world around us play a key role. Throwing a ball implies, within the muscle movement of the arms (and according to the predictive processing account), a series of predictions on how high and far the ball is going to go, even before the projectile has reached this point in its trajectory. When we swing our arms back and forth in preparation of a throw, we adjust our muscle movements to fit to the optimal predictions once we actually release the ball. Such predictions are much more precise in expert throwers (say, for example, professional cricketers), and they develop through repeated practice and imitation. Arguably, for female throwers, who are habituated to a constrained bodily experience through female dress and ideal comportment, the predictions that inform the throw (and hence the throw itself) will be vastly different. Within the predictive processing account, female throwers are not condemned to remain constrained, however, because conscious practice can recalibrate predictions and lead to more powerful throws in female athletes. Yet the issue remains that in everyday contexts female role models provide practice and entrainment in a more constrained, female mode of movement.

The embodied experience of the world and our sense of the options to take action within it (that is, our very perception of the world in the embodied cognition account), then becomes profoundly dependent on the predictions derived from templates of male or female comportment that have been engrained for years. Culture and cognition cannot be separated once we acknowledge that embodied experience is something which does not emerge ineffably between bodies and the environment, but that, dependent on developing predictions, it is shaped by our muscle memory of movement and the feedback of our physical, social and mediated environment on our performance of this movement.

Predictive processing is a comparatively young strand in the cognitive sciences and philosophy of mind, and the debates, in particular with respect to the role and importance of embodiment, are ongoing.[17] In what follows, I shall assume that the embodied and embedded dimension of predictive processing cannot be separated from its probabilistic dimension. To my mind, it is exactly the dialogue and feedback between embodied experience and the expectations that prefigure, shape and make it meaningful that constitutes the strength of embodied predictive processing for the analysis of cultural phenomena, such as literary narrative and it can be profitably developed in this respect in dialogue with feminist critiques of embodiment.

Simone de Beauvoir, in *The Second Sex*, famously writes 'One is not born, but rather becomes, a woman.'[18] As Sonia Kruks points out, this phrase presents the female experience as 'situated' in a particular bodily and social context and it 'denaturalises' it at the same time.[19] Femininity is a constructed category, but it nevertheless forms part of the lived experience of the female subject (also De Beauvoir draws on Merleau-Ponty), and 'subjectivity is corporally constituted; it is co-extensive with the body, while being simultaneously a "point of view"'.[20] In what follows, I shall explore three different avenues for an embodied cognitive narratology from this Beauvoirean perspective, as one 'becomes' a woman through the performance of such a gender role, through the living of a particular habitus and through the interpellation of others to assume a recognisable position in intersubjective exchanges.

The term 'performance' is a difficult one with respect to the way in which embodied predictive processing plays out in everyday cognition. The permutations which the term underwent in the work of Judith Butler from *Gender Trouble* (1990) to *Bodies That Matter* (1993), for example, are indicative of the tensions between empowerment and constraints in gendered, embodied actions which are necessary, I think, to develop the full versatility of embodied cognition. While the throwing of a ball is quite clearly a performance in the sense that the potential of movement is actualised in the world in a particular style and manner, it does not necessarily mean that this performance is 'theatrical' in the sense that we assume a role, consciously and with deliberation. The performance of embodied actions can arguably be changed through conscious practice, but it usually cannot be assumed and discarded with the same ease and detachment that one associates with a theatrical role. Furthermore, the predictive, probabilistic models of embodied and social cognition, which shape our expectations, are not discursive in the sense that they can be confined to the realm of social and linguistic constructions. They are a model of the world that develops in constant interaction with physical and cultural feedback from this world. In that sense, predictive processing is anchored in the body just as much as in the cultural scripts and roles, with no notion of a separate 'discourse'. 'Performance' in this context can take a range of meanings, from deliberate, practised and creatively appropriating to automatic, preconscious and constrained, depending on how, in each individual case, the feedback loop between embodied experience and the probabilistic predictions is configured. The state of 'becoming', in this model of embodied predictive processing, can remain in flux.

Habitus is most closely connected with the work of Pierre Bourdieu and his analysis of embodied social practices, where the entrained actions of the individual demonstrate his belonging to a particular group such as a social class or an ethnic community. Bourdieu, to my knowledge, does not discuss gender in particular, but arguably, there is a gendered dimension to the embodied practice of habitus that cuts, in intersectional fashion, across class.[21] The narrator and the assassin in Mantel, for example, constantly size each other up in terms of their social class and it is the attention to detail, as in Bourdieu's analyses of habitus as social practice, that brings such larger social formations to the fore.[22] The narrator assesses the assassin as one of 'those who were bright enough to say "affinity", but still wore cheap nylon coats' (p. 273), that is, a working-class man who was not given equal educational and professional opportunities as her own middle-class self. At the same time, the fact that she can only offer demerara sugar for his tea, marks her out as a member of the 'bourgeoisie' for him (p. 272). Language, dress, and food habits carry clear social markers that become invisible within one's own social class. Habitus also extends into the way in which characters shape their environment through embodied interaction. Even though the narrator realises that she has an assassin in her drawing room, she still feels the need to be a proper middle-class hostess, and Mantel chooses to point this out in her gestures in this world. She drags the duvet over her unmade bed 'to tidy it' (p. 265), she prepares tea for him and is 'flustered by a failing in hospitality' when he comments on the sugar missing from his tea (p. 272).

The lived habitus of the narrator includes a very embodied way of engaging with and organising her surroundings, as well as her choice of words. The character 'becomes' a woman, and more specifically a middle-class woman, through both actions and language. Gender-oriented sociolinguistics (I am thinking in particular of Deborah Cameron's *Verbal Hygiene* [1995]) and the embodied approach in cognitive linguistics are arguably compatible from this point of view. The language that is used does not only reflect that way in which we conceptualise the world around us, it also provides the very means of conceptualisation when we think of cognition as grounded in the human body. On the one hand, it seems that a sense of bodily relations, distances and modes of movement underlie the metaphors and situated conceptualisations which we express in language, our bodies shape the way in which we express abstract thoughts in language.[23] On the other hand, it seems that the embodied patterns and models of language, in particular as it is given in socio-typical language use, prefigure (as a predictive, probabilistic model) our very perception of the world and, by extension, our understanding of ourselves and our social contexts.[24] And of course, language is often heavily gendered. For example, even though in 'The Assassination of Margaret Thatcher' Mantel does not specify explicitly that her narrator is female, the moment when she describes herself as 'flustered over a failing in hospitality' makes it relatively clear that the voice narrating the encounter is a woman's. The verb 'flustered' describes a state of the body and mind which is particularly gendered as female and it is part of the embodied habitus of the middle-class woman, predicting how she should feel in a particular situation and, in turn, giving conceptual shape to this particular bodily experience when it occurs.

The performance of gender roles and the lived practice of the habitus are complemented by the way in which this embodied experience of the world gains a normative dimension through Althusserian interpellation. As the narrator in Mantel's 'The Assassination of Margaret Thatcher' makes clear, Thatcher does not simply perform a gender role. Instead, her looks are perceived as an accusation of the insufficiency of other looks and a summons to imitate her (and thus become relatable by her standards). The narrator explains to the assassin,

> 'Mind you,' I said, 'she'd probably laugh if she were here. She'd laugh because she despises us. Look at your anorak. She despises your anorak. Look at my hair. She despises my hair.'

> He glanced up. He'd not looked at me before, not to see me; I was just the tea-maker. 'The way it just hangs there,' I explained. 'Instead of being in corrugations. I ought to have it washed and set. It ought to go in graduated rollers, she knows where she is with that sort of hair.' (p. 274)

The narrator draws attention to her performance of the female gender role and how closely it is related to others' normative expectations and demands. She is certain that Thatcher 'despises' her hair because it is not pressed and controlled by the technologies of coiffure as is her own. The narrator does not look as she feels she 'ought' to look by the standards of Margaret Thatcher and hence experiences the interpellation of 'corrugations' and 'graduated rollers'.

Mantel provides another mock-heroic moment in her short story here, as she relates Thatcher's will to dominate through her well-controlled looks and the need to 'know where she is with that sort of hair'. At the same time, however, she points to an important aspect of the embodied female experience at the point where interpellation and objectification are linked. Young in 'Throwing Like a Girl' suggests that the inhibition of female throwers is to do with the fact that they do not direct their attention to 'what we want to do *through* our bodies' but rather 'must have our attention directed upon our bodies'. The female body, so Young, is *'looked at and acted upon'*.[25] The issue of gendered body images, in other words, is not only to do with the different predictive models available to different genders but also with the degree to which the predictive model and its performance is regarded and assessed from a third-person perspective. The narrator sees Thatcher through her accessories, the handbag and the hairdo, because that is how she herself judges her and feels to be judged by her. The felt reliability of the feedback loop between embodied experience and predictive, probabilistic modes now comes to the fore. This is what the predictive processing approach calls 'precision'.[26] For Mantel's narrator, the reliability of her own body image and that of Thatcher is a problem to be considered, whereas for the assassin, it is not. It is not my intention to claim that men do not experience interpellation of this kind; I merely mean to point out how Mantel differentiates between the embodied experience of the narrator and the assassin along these lines of 'becoming' as well.

The basic assumption that mind and body work together in meaning-making has been complicated beyond the distinction of 'body image' and 'body schema' in several respects now, and we have three dimensions along which an embodied cognitive narratology can engage with questions of gender. First, the feedback loop between embodied experience and the environment can be configured in different ways, ranging from greater agency of the individual to create one's predictive models (that is, performance as theatre) to greater constraints from the predictive models on individual behaviour (that is, performance as control). By tracing how the embodied actions and perceptions (as mentioned in the narrative text) are related to these larger expectations, cognitive narratologists can reconstruct the relative balance of this feedback loop and come to an assessment of the gendered differences in characters' experiences of their body image and their options for actions in the environment of the storyworld. Second, the relation between language and action can be used to work out the gendered habitus of the characters and to assess how the storyworld is turned into a lifeworld. The traditional notion of narratological storyworld captures the relations of characters with each other and their interactions, leading to a plot. When the storyworld shifts into a lifeworld, this also allows for a reflection on how these relations and interactions are shaped by embodied habitus. Third, the way in which narration communicates the reliability of these feedback loops yields patterns of interpellation and objectification for characters, narrators and readers. In each of these dimensions, however, the embodied experience of gender-specific 'becoming' cannot be made independent of the body in an abstract realm of 'discourse' or 'construction'.

3. The embodied edge

Up until now, I have presented the predictive processing model as it applies to real-world cognitive embodied processes, in parallel with the words and actions of the characters in the text. However, Mantel's short story 'The Assassination of Margaret Thatcher' is an entirely verbal construct; a representation and not the real world. It has been argued, convincingly, I think, that reading a written text depends on the embodied resonances of readers to motion verbs, directions and the descriptions of bodily states. Readers make sense of the words on the page through the way in which they feel them in their own bodies. Reading might not be exclusively dependent on such resonances but it is profoundly embodied.[27] At the same time, however, literary mimesis is one step removed from experiences and interactions in the real world through the mediation of language and writing.

This mediation in language and writing, as I have argued elsewhere,[28] enables literary narrative to highlight aspects of our everyday lived bodies that remain invisible in the flow of real-world experience. In a conversation in the streets of Windsor, before the visit of the assassin, the narrator has the following exchange with a stranger about the visit from the prime minister.

> She said, 'There are some strong opinions flying about.'
>
> 'Mine is a dagger,' I said, 'and it's flying straight to her heart.' (p. 258)

Strictly speaking, the exchange is based on a conceptual metaphor according to which an abstract element (that is, 'opinion') is characterised by a concrete, potentially embodied activity (that is, 'flying about').[29] Such combinations are ubiquitous in everyday conversations and we usually pay no heed to their embodied dimension, even though it underpins the way in which we understand these expressions (if conceptual metaphor theory is right). However, in this example from Mantel, the concrete, potentially embodied activity of 'flying about' regains its embodied edge when the 'opinion' is turned into a 'dagger' that is 'flying straight to her heart'. The embodied resonances of the motion verb are underlined when the projectile gains physical shape and when it is given a trajectory into the vital organs of Margaret Thatcher.

In this little exchange, Mantel brings out the embodied resonances that underlie the understanding of language by turning them into concrete objects in her storyworld and thus foregrounding the predictions that shape our embodied experience and make it relatable in its attendant language use. As literary language draws attention to the (seemingly) predictable embodied experiences of its characters and narrators, it performs the double-function of (1) showing how much we are rooted in our lived bodies and of (2) denaturalising the social and cultural scripts within which our embodied experience is inevitably situated. As Mantel's narrator places her Perrier water in the fridge, remarks on the cheap nylon jacket of the assassin and gets 'flustered' over her short-comings in hospitality, this could all be natural enough. In Mantel's short story, however, we find her playing through the embodied habitus of the middle-class woman while an assassin sits in her living room and she serves him tea. Does the narrator simply lack the capacity to assume any other kind of agency? Does Mantel make a statement about the underlying dispassionateness of playing social roles? Or does the habitus of the middle-class woman also serve as a protective shell in this encounter with an assassin? In the fictional situation, these elements of habitus gain an embodied edge, too, with the dispassionate perspective on the body images that the narrator insists on.

Throughout Mantel's 'The Assassination of Margaret Thatcher', the everyday lived experience of gendered and social realities in Windsor is heightened, be it through literalised metaphors in the discourse, be it through the mock-heroic elements in its treatment of Thatcher or be it through the incongruity of the situation with the assassin drinking tea in the middle-class living room. Literary mimesis consistently draws attention to the relationship between the embodied experience and the cultural and social templates which inform its probabilities in the feedback loop of predictive processing. It gives the immersive dimension of literary reading, intensity and, depending on embodied resonances, a defamiliarising moment. Indeed, in the dialogue cited above, the embodied edge translates into the very development of the plot, which introduces a character about to pull the trigger in the midst of these 'strong opinions flying about'. With the parallel between the dagger-like opinion of the narrator and the physical bullet of the assassin, Mantel underlines the ways in which language and bodily experience shape each other. The narrative ends just before the assassination, where the verbal embodiment is about to be translated into physical events, as Thatcher comes into view. In the novella itself, Mantel's literary language keeps them in an uneasy, provocative balance.

My brief analytical snap-shots of 'The Assassination of Margaret Thatcher' give only some examples of how an embodied cognitive narratology can approach the moving target of a feminist perspective. It depends on the embodied predictive processing model of cognition, which includes both the phenomenological notion of the lived body in its surroundings and the probabilistic notion of likely scripts and templates which inform the ways in which this lived body is played out. Neither on the side of phenomenology nor on the side of cultural templates can such embodied narratology do without the gender perspective. A feminist cognitive analyse reveals how, in 'The Assassination of Margaret Thatcher', Mantel makes an assault on preconceived notions of gender and class through the double dimension of embodiment and prediction.

***

Close to the end of 'The Assassination of Margaret Thatcher', Mantel speaks of a 'the door in the wall' (p. 285). 'It is a special door and obeys no laws that govern wood or iron. No locksmith can defeat it, no bailiff kick it in; patrolling policemen pass it, because it is visible only to the eye of faith' (p. 285). Mantel's short story is such as 'door in the wall'. We know that Margaret Thatcher was not assassinated in the spring of 1983, even though Mantel's narrative begins with the sentence, 'Picture first the street where she breathed her last' (p. 253). Mantel takes us into a storyworld that is 'visible only to the eye of faith', and while it follows the general logic of the door in that we can pass throw its threshold from one world to another, as she says, it 'obeys no laws that govern wood or iron'. Perhaps we can extend this metaphor to develop a view for an embodied cognitive feminist narratology. The cascades of cognition involved in the embodied reading of literature do not simply reproduce the gendered realities, cognitive, embodied or otherwise, of the world around us. They do not 'obey the laws' of the real world. Rather they realise the full potential of gendered metaphors, expectations of comportment and invisible habitus in literary language: to reflect on the experience and its underlying predictions while you live it. An embodied feminist narratology can offer a perspective on how literature enables embodied immersion in fictional worlds while carrying the potential to make readers feel the embodied edge of historical, political and gendered situatedness.

Notes

1. Hilary Mantel, 'The Assassination of Margaret Thatcher', in *The Assassination of Margaret Thatcher* (London: Fourth Estate, 2014), pp. 248–88. At the time of writing this article (9 May 2016), the MLA International Bibliography lists no more than 26 entries on Mantel's substantial oeuvre (and 11 of these entries refer not to academic articles but to book reviews and interviews). Compare this to Ian McEwan's 416 entries, Julian Barnes's 236 entries or Martin Amis's 203 entries.
2. For the basic references to cognitive narratology drawn on here, see David Herman, *Storylogic: Problems and Possibilities of Narrative* (Lincoln: University of Nebraska Press, 2002); Marie-Laure Ryan, *Possible Worlds, Artificial Intelligence and Narrative* (Bloomington: Indiana University Press, 1991); Monika Fludernik, *Toward a 'Natural' Narratology* (London: Routledge, 1996); Lisa Zunshine, *Why We Read Fiction* (Columbus: Ohio State University Press, 2007); Blakey Vermeule, *Why Do We Care About Literary Characters* (Baltimore, MD: Johns Hopkins University Press, 2010); and Alan Palmer, *Fictional Minds* (Lincoln: University of Nebraska Press, 2004).
3. See Susan Lanser, *Fictions of Authority: Women Writers and Narrative Voice* (Ithaca, NY: Cornell University Press, 1992) and Robyn Warhol, *Having a Good Cry Effeminate Feelings and Pop Culture Forms* (Columbus: Ohio State University Press, 2003) for examples of feminist treatments of narration, emotional engagements and plot types. Hilary Dannenberg, *Coincidence and*

Counterfactuality: Plotting Time and Space in Narrative Fiction (Lincoln: University of Nebraska Press, 2008) is a good example of how cognitive and gender perspectives can be fruitfully combined, but this remains the exception in cognitive narratology.
4. Simon Baron-Cohen, *The Essential Difference: Forget Mars and Venus and Discover the Truth about the Opposite Sex* (London: Penguin, 2004).
5. See Lisa Zunshine, *Why We Read Fiction: Theory of Mind and the Novel* (Columbus: Ohio State University Press, 2008) and *Getting Inside Your Head: What Cognitive Science Can Tell Us about Cognitive Culture* (Baltimore, MD: Johns Hopkins University Press, 2012), as well as the contributions in Paula Leverage et al. (eds.), *Theory of Mind and Literature* (Ashland, OH: Purdue University Press, 2014). Kay Young, 'Sex – Text – Cortex', in Susan Lanser and Robyn Warhol (eds.), *Narrative Theory Unbound: Queer and Feminist Interventions* (Columbus: Ohio State University Press, 2016), pp. 312–22 rightly points out the need to engage with brain science from the point of view of feminist narratology but then focuses on the critique of the approach rather than an integrated model.
6. For the term 'neurosexism', see Robyn Bluhm, 'Beyond Neurosexism: Is it Possible to Defend the Female Brain?', in Robyn Bluhm, Anne Jaap Jakobson and Heidi Lene Maibom (eds.), *Neurofeminism: Issues at the Intersection of Feminist Theory and Cognitive Science* (Houndsmills, Basingstoke: Palgrave Macmillan, 2012), pp. 230–45. Further articles in this volume question recent research suggesting that male and female brains show significant differences; Giordana Grossi and Cordelia Fine, 'The Role of Fetal Testosterone in the Development of the "Essential Difference" Between the Sexes: Some Essential Issues', in Robyn Bluhm, Anne Jaap Jakobson and Heidi Lene Maibom (eds.), *Neurofeminism: Issues at the Intersection of Feminist Theory and Cognitive Science* (Houndsmills, Basingstoke: Palgrave Macmillan, 2012), pp. 73–104, give a trenchant critique of Baron-Cohen's distinctions. For a classical rebuttal of research on the 'corpus callosum' (that connects the two hemispheres and is supposedly more prominent in the female brain), see Anne Fausto-Sterling, *Sexing the Body: Gender Politics and the Construction of Sexuality* (New York: Basic Books, 2000), particularly ch. 5. 'Sexing the Brain: How Biologists Make a Difference'.
7. David Herman, James Phelan, Peter J. Rabinowitz, Brian Richardson and Robyn Warhol, *Narrative Theory: Core Concepts and Critical Debates* (Columbus: Ohio State University Press, 2012), p. 10.
8. Ibid. 210; for Herman's response, see pp. 220–2.
9. Herman mentions Andy Clark, *Supersizing the Mind: Embodiment, Action and Cognitive Extension* (Oxford: Oxford University Press, 2008); J. J. Gibson, *An Ecological Approach to Visual Perception* (Boston, MA: Houghton-Mifflin, 1979) and Alva Noë, *Action in Perception* (Cambridge, MA: MIT Press, 2004).
10. See Chris Frith, *Making up the Mind: How the Brain Creates our Mental World* (Oxford: Wiley-Blackwell, 2007) and Andy Clark, 'Whatever Next? Predictive Brains, Situated Agents, and the Future of Cognitive Science', *Brain and Behavioral Sciences*, 36, no. 3 (2013), pp. 181–204 for accessible introductions to predictive processing.
11. In what follows, references to this short story will be made in parentheses in the main text.

12. Quotation ascribed to Thatcher in an article discussing the term 'handbagging'. Ollie Stone-Lee, 'I Was Handbagged by Margaret Thatcher', *BBC News* (9 April 2013), http://www.bbc.com/news/uk-politics-11518330.
13. See Shaun Gallagher, *How the Body Shapes the Mind* (Oxford: Oxford University Press, 2008) for this distinction.
14. A broad range of neuropsychological and philosophical accounts of how these different levels of embodied are interconnected has emerged in recent years. See Marco Caracciolo and Karin Kukkonen (eds.), *Cognitive Literary Study: Second-Generation Perspectives* (special issue of *Style*, 48, no. 3, 2014) for an overview on this literature and a series of contributions that consider how elements of literary criticism can be reconceptualised through the different dimensions of embodied cognition.
15. Karin Kukkonen, 'Presence and Prediction: The Embodied Reader's Cascades of Cognition', *Style*, 48, no. 3 (2014), pp. 367–84.
16. Iris Marion Young, 'Throwing Like a Girl: A Phenomenology of Feminine Body Comportment, Mobility and Spatiality', in *The Female Body Experience: 'Throwing Like a Girl' and other Essays* (Oxford: Oxford University Press, 2005), p. 33.
17. See Andy Clark, *Surfing Uncertainty: Prediction, Action and the Embodied Mind* (Oxford: Oxford University Press, 2016) and Jakob Hohwy, *The Predictive Mind* (Oxford: Oxford University Press, 2013) for two key statements in the debate. Clark sees predictive processing as irrevocably rooted in the body, while Hohwy conceptualises the predictive dimension as separable from embodied experience.
18. Simone de Beauvoir, *The Second Sex* (Harmondsworth: Penguin, 1983 [1949]), p. 295.
19. See Sonia Kruks, 'Gender and Subjectivity: Simone de Beauvoir and Contemporary Feminism', *Signs: Journal of Women in Culture and Society*, 18, no. 1 (1992), pp. 89–110.
20. Kruks, 'Gender and Subjectivity', p. 107.
21. See Toril Moi, 'Appropriating Bourdieu: Feminist Theory and Pierre Bourdieu's Sociology of Culture', *New Literary History*, 22, no.4 (1991), pp. 1019–49 for an argument introducing Bourdieu in feminist studies.
22. See especially, Pierre Bourdieu, *Practical Reason: On the Theory of Action* (Cambridge: Polity, 1998) and Pierre Bourdieu, *Outline of a Theory of Praxis* (Cambridge: Cambridge University Press, 1977).
23. See for example Raymond Gibbs, *Embodiment and Cognitive Science* (Cambridge: Cambridge University Press, 2005) and Lawrence Barsalou, 'Grounded Cognition', *Annual Review of Psychology*, 59 (2008), pp. 617–45.
24. See Benjamin Bergen, *Louder than Words: The New Science of How the Mind Makes Meaning* (Washington, DC: Basic Books, 2012) for a popularised, comprehensive introduction to this approach. Gary Lupyan and Andy Clark, 'Words and the World: Predictive Coding and the Language-Perception-Cognition Interface', *Current Directions in Psychological Science*, 24, no. 4 (2015), pp. 279–84 provide an up-to-date predictive processing perspective on these issues.
25. Young, 'Throwing like a Girl', p. 34 and 39.
26. Kukkonen, 'Presence and Prediction', p. 375.
27. See Bergen, *Louder than Words*, for an outline of such embodied reading. The notion that readers experience an embodied resonance of what they read about

is at the core of cognitive approaches to literature that depend on embodied cognition, such as Guillemette Bolens, *The Style of Gestures: Embodiment and Literary Narrative* (Baltimore, MD: Johns Hopkins, 2012) and Marco Caracciolo, *The Experientiality of Narrative: An Enactivist Approach* (Berlin: DeGruyter, 2014).
28. Karin Kukkonen, 'Bayesian Bodies: The Predictive Dimension of Embodied Cognition and Culture', in Peter Garrett (ed.), *The Embodied Mind in Culture* (London: Palgrave Macmillan, 2016), pp. 153–66.
29. See George Lakoff and Mark Johnson, *Metaphors We Live By* (Chicago, IL: University of Chicago Press, 1980) for the classical account on conceptual metaphors.

Acknowledgements

I would like to thank Susan Lanser and Tory Young for their excellent comments on earlier versions of this article.

Disclosure statement

No potential conflict of interest was reported by the author.

Funding

This work was supported by the Academy of Finland under grant 267599 (How the Novel Found its Feet: Embodiment and Eighteenth-Century Fiction).

Invisibility and power in the digital age: issues for feminist and queer narratology

Tory Young

ABSTRACT
This essay examines the continued assumption that representational visibility equates to power, in the digital age. It considers the tension between the image as a form that captures what already exists and the image as a future possibility in the era of the mantra 'You cannot be what you cannot see' and growing recognition of gender fluidity. After re-examination of Peggy Phelan's reminder about the power of the unmarked, I turn to Ali Smith's 2014 *How to be both*, a novel with an interchangeable Renaissance narrative and contemporary story in a palimpsestic structure, to propose a formula that could be described as the *becoming-simultaneous of narrative sequence*. In conceiving the 'unnarrated' as both a gap in what was represented in retrospect in an existing storyworld but equally as a narrative future, I link the unmarked to political possibility, and conclude that you cannot always see what you can be.

'If representational visibility equals power' Peggy Phelan wrote in 1993, 'then almost-naked young white women should be running Western culture'.[1] This outright challenge to the equivalence of visibility and power, for all its power and wit, has not managed to dislodge what is a settled assumption in much feminist theory, and in more general thinking about the relationship between representation and politics: that representational visibility is a positive value in itself. There is, in other words, an established view that the question of visibility itself is more basic than questions of how something is represented since visibility itself confers membership of the known universe on a particular social identity. To be able to see something or someone, in the sphere of representation, is to know that it is possible within what Phelan calls the 'boundaries of the putative real' (p. 1). This is an assumption that underlies many feminist positions, slogans and popular injunctions that take visibility as a political issue. A contemporary example is *Miss Representation*, an internet project with the explicit aim of increasing the number of women working in positions of power, in science, technology, commerce and industry, which upholds the view that aspirational possibility is founded in representational visibility under the formula 'You can't be what you can't see.'[2] Marian Wright Edelman's mantra is used more widely in social media to apply to the representation of other marginalised groups, to inspire the isolated individual and show her that she is not alone in her sexuality, race, interests, or professional ambition. Her slogan is aspirational; it is postfeminist, in appealing to the individual's motivation to achieve, rather than feminist, which would consider the structures of oppression that prevent her from doing so. It establishes a basic equivalence between what is possible and what can be seen, but it also, crucially, places a responsibility on the makers of the image to present the marginalised in a good light, as role models, and so avoids the crude equation of visibility and power. This tension between representational visibility itself and positive value, which was at the heart of Phelan's project in 1993, will be a framework for the discussion of contemporary fiction that follows. I use Ali Smith's 2014 novel *How to be both* to propose a new dimension to the dynamic relationship between narrative and sexuality of spatialised form, whilst simultaneously reconsidering Phelan in the current digital era.

It might be argued that the equivalence of visibility with power belongs to a new presupposition that pervades the internet, and which inverts the relationship between events and their representation. 'Pics or it didn't happen' is the more banal cry of the Instagram era, which declares that without visual documentation on social media an event did not occur at all.[3] Like Edelman's call, it affirms the power of the visible; what can be seen is what matters, what can be seen is what is real. In the classical concept of mimesis, reality comes first and representation follows, but the power bestowed on the representation of the visible in the internet age seems to distort or challenge this order. 'Pics or it didn't happen' encapsulates a strange inversion of events and representations that has become a refrain in literary and cultural theory concerned to show that words, and representations in general, construct rather than reflect social reality. But no theory is involved, no structuralist linguistics or performative speech acts needed, in this statement of the primordial visual image. It evokes Derrida's account of the archive, as something which produces as much as it records the event, or Stiegler's account of the originary externalisation of memory, but it does so at the level of the snap, on the platform of social media.[4] The tension between representation and aspiration in Edelman's statement 'you can't be what you can't see' can also be understood in these terms, as a tension between the image as a form that captures what already exists, and the image as a future possibility (i.e. you cannot become what is not visible in representation). The tendency in the visual image to point backwards and forwards, the queer temporality that inverts the relationship between the before and after, surfaces in various ways in the analysis of vision and visibility below. In different ways, the issue of visibility's equivalence to power is transformed by this temporal queerness, into a question about which comes first, or more specifically, whether visual representation can produce, as well as reflect, political power.

I. The unmarked

Phelan is not, of course, arguing against media representation of marginalised groups, but outlining the problems of any straightforward belief that heightened visibility might lead to social inclusion or power. One such problem is the assumption that visual appearance has the power to represent a coherent community or social identity at all. In a recent interview, Maggie Nelson illustrates this problem in what we might call the Caitlyn Jenner paradox: '[t]he most shocking thing about Caitlyn Jenner is that she's a Republican. That's proof alone that it's not clear what politics stem from certain gender and sexuality arrangements'.[5] Jenner is a high-profile transgender woman, whose attendance at Donald Trump's Inauguration prevents feelings of kinship from most other transgender women. This self-evident multiplicity of things, the heterogeneity of entities and identities, nevertheless continues to trouble the representation of marginalised groups whose composition by individuals and differences is so often erased by what Phelan refers to as 'identity politics'. The paradox that comes into view is that the recognition of an identity or community in the public sphere erases the composition of that identity by individuals, while any undue emphasis on individuality will fragment, factionalise and weaken the collective identity that is addressed.

These are old and familiar problems in the logic of sameness and difference for political action. Phelan's main argument with the simplifications of identity politics concern sight, what can and cannot be seen, what can and cannot be known. We cannot necessarily see a category of person. We do not always recognise a community. We cannot necessarily categorise a person. If we cannot always see another's gender, sexuality, race or politics, Phelan argues, it is 'unmarked' and there is therefore no 'smoothly mimetic' (p. 7) link between representation and identity. Instead, Phelan claims that each of these 'presumption[s] reflects the ideology of the visible, an ideology which erases the power of the unmarked, unspoken, and unseen' (p. 7). Phelan's aim is to unpick the perceived 'binary between the power of visibility and the impotency of invisibility', to assert the 'real power in remaining unmarked' and point out that 'Visibility is a trap [...]; it summons surveillance and the law; it provokes voyeurism, fetishism, the colonialist/imperial appetite for possession' (p. 6). In this argument then, the equivalence between power and visibility is displaced by the opposite view, that invisibility might be a locus of power. For Phelan, 'you can't be what you can't see' equates that which is real with that which is visible, fixing the identity into one flawed image.

Phelan asks us to recognise just how unorthodox a thought this is – that we might value the immaterial or the invisible – in the current climate. It is exactly this unorthodox alignment of power with the invisible or unmarked that I want to develop and amplify here. The urgency of this plea has, in my view, only increased in the twenty-first century, in the context of a culture that relies ever more heavily on visible representation and affirms the visible as that which is real. In her article on trans narratives for the *London Review of Books*, Jacqueline Rose notes of Caitlyn Jenner's famous *Vanity Fair* cover that '[i]t's as if [...] the photographic session, rather than hormones or surgery, were the culmination of the process (though Liebovitz herself insists that the photos were secondary to the project of helping Caitlyn to "emerge")'.[6] In this sense of the true self being fixed and externalised in the realm of representation, rather than in the interior of the subject, we find the same inversion of the before and after, and the same entanglement of reality and its image, that preside over the question of visibility and power.

II. Feminist narratology and the unseen

What can be seen, who is seen and who sees, have long been questions of concern to feminists. Groundbreaking work in theories of spectatorship (by Mary Ann Doane, Laura Mulvey, Jacqueline Rose) employed psychoanalysis to posit a male gaze as the default position in film, and even culture at large. But in her 1996 essay on looking and *Persuasion*, Robyn Warhol claimed that 'narratology has not made as much use as it might of the notion of the "gaze" as it has developed in film studies'.[7] This was all the more surprising for the fact that, as Warhol goes on to say, 'the gaze in film and the focalization of verbal texts are similar in their function'.[8] In the volume of essays Warhol and Susan S. Lanser edited in 2013, *Narrative Theory Unbound: Queer and Feminist Interventions*, Lanser, reflecting upon developments in feminist narratology since her 1986 inaugurating essay, 'Toward a Feminist Narratology', demonstrates that her gendered theorising of focalisation (who sees) and narrative voice (who speaks) are the significant achievements of this strand of post-classical narratology:

> A still queerer lens might suggest that when a heterodiegetic narrator's gender is unmarked, heterodiegesis becomes the very emblem of gender indeterminacy. We're all doubtless familiar as teachers with the students who say, 'in this novel *it* says ... '; perhaps that is not simply a sign of ignorance, as I have certainly lamented on more than one occasion, but a sign of queerness, and historical instability, of heterodiegesis itself.[9]

Lanser's graduation from working towards a more feminist narratology to working towards a queerer narratology since 1986 reflects the rise of queer theory and growing recognition of the need for intersectionality in that time; no longer can a single identity category stand as a satisfactory means of investigating experience and representation. The notion of gender fluidity, signified in Lanser's account by the pronoun 'it' in narrative, has also become more prominent, even mainstream, in the twenty-first century. Does 'it' represent the power of Phelan's unseen? What problems does 'it' therefore present for mimetic representation?

One optimistic reading of Lanser's account is that there is no problem: that what texts and readers have always already known is now being disclosed and foregrounded by narratologists and gender theorists. For Lanser, 'heterodiegesis [may be] the very emblem of gender indeterminacy'.[10] Thus, the narrative representation of fluid genders is as old as the novel itself, in the sense that novels have always recognised and dramatised social aspects of voice, including gender indeterminacies, that may not be fully acknowledged or understood in the 'outside' world. The novel, in this sense, may always have been at work on the complications of gender fluidity and the unmarked voice in ways that affirm again the basic thesis that representations might, at times, be thought of as anterior and not posterior to the behaviours they describe or the actions they imitate.

I would like to propose that a step can be taken in the same direction with the help of what might be called 'spatialised form': a kind of dynamic movement between spatial arrangement and narrative sequence, that, like indeterminate gender voices, queers the distinction between space and time. The becoming time of space and becoming space of time is, I would like to propose, with Martin Hägglund, an inherent property of narrative sequence, exploited by novels for particular thematic purposes.[11] My interest in this dynamic conflation is that it can be taken as another core formal property of narrative, and one which co-operates with the entanglements of voice, sometimes in the service of a kind of queering. In the remainder of this essay, I would like to explore, in particular, Ali Smith's 2014 novel *How to be both* to develop the idea that spatialised form can contribute to our understanding of the erotics of narrative, and at the same time specify the ways in which a novel itself can conduct an enquiry into the topic of visibility and power.[12]

III. *How to be both* and spatialised form

Ali Smith's novel *How to be both* is composed of two parts, which have become known as 'Camera' and 'Eyes', after the line drawings which precede each respectively. The camera is a surveillance camera; the eyes are on a stalk, extracted from a painting of St. Lucy by the Italian Renaissance painter, Francesco del Cossa (c.1430–c.1477). 'Camera' tells the story of a present-day teenager, George (short for Georgia), who lives in Cambridge and whose mother Carol has recently and suddenly died. Shortly before her death, Carol, fascinated by an image painted by del Cossa that she stumbled upon in a magazine, took George and her brother Henry to see it 'for real' in Ferrara (p. 233). 'Eyes' gives a fictionalised account of del Cossa's life, in which 'he' is a woman disguised as a man to enable a career as a painter. In this outline, the thematics of vision can already be understood in their Shakespearean relation to gender, but also in the historical zoning of the novel's action between the Renaissance and the digital gaze.

Another level of vision is foregrounded by *How to be both*, namely the act of looking at words on a page. Readers, especially those who are unfamiliar with modernism, can find Smith's prose challenging exactly because her books are visually striking: sometimes words are presented as concrete or pattern poems, with puzzling typographical significance and/or onomatopoeic resonance. Here is an example from page 4:

just caught my (what)

on a (ouch)

dodged a (whew) (biff)

(bash) (ow)

(mercy)

On first sight, there appears to be a lot of white space on each page, even when a narrative sequence rather than a poetic pattern is given; closer investigation reveals that this is partly because the text is not justified, typographically aligned. Words are not broken up and hyphenated to fill a line and the text is not therefore dense or full. This unusual presentation is enhanced by a range of other visual and graphic properties. There are no inverted commas around speech but there is a space before as well as after a colon, and many colons are used;

and that over there, that's him, isn't it? Never

seen it before but it's him : yes : ah : it's a beauty :

and that one there's him too, is it? (p. 9)

Our experience of reading then is to be struck by visual differences, some of which we cannot initially explain. Whilst the absence of speech marks is readily identified, the unjustified text is not. I would argue that Smith's spatial presentation makes us see what is usually present but is absent in her texts; the blank spaces perform the power of the unseen.

These are typographical features of all Smith's books since *Hotel World* in 2001, but what is most surprising about *How to be both* is that it was printed in two formats; it is entirely accidental whether the reader gets 'Camera' or 'Eyes' first.[13] Each part is labelled 'One', so even if a reader is unaware that chance has determined the order in which she receives the book, reaching another part 'One' half-way through indicates a challenge to linear chronology. Each part 'One' has the quality of a palimpsest to the other; Francescho [*sic*] haunts 'Camera', watching George, whilst 'Eyes' may have been focalised or written by George (as hinted by the different spelling of the artist's name and the repetition of the anachronistic teenage idiom 'just saying' throughout). These connections and the absence of sequence resulting from the two part Ones inspire the reader to re-read the book at least one more time to understand the links; thus an ending is perpetually deferred and the beginning and ends of each section overlap. Within each part, chronology is further disrupted: in 'Camera', George's memories of her mother and her current life are presented simultaneously; Carol is both dead and alive. As I shall show, there are countless instances of doubling and simultaneity, of bothness, throughout. In the interchangeability of the Renaissance narrative with the contemporary story, and in the palimpsest structure, the novel places the before and after of chronology into a dynamic relation that conflates the then and the now of historical time, in a formula that could be described as the *becoming-simultaneous of narrative sequence*.

The visual surface of language constantly comes into view as part of the thematics of before and after in *How to be both*. At the start of the 'Camera' version (i.e. that half of the print run that begins with Camera), there is a scene focalised by George in which she recalls a conversation with her mother, Carol, in the present tense. They are in the car in Italy 'last May' on the way to visit the Ferrara frieze. Carol, who is the anonymous author of 'Subverts', politically subversive texts which pop up on art websites and artistic texts which pop up on political websites (one of the many examples of simultaneity in the novel), asks George a question about moral integrity relating to del Cossa's demands for a higher rate of pay for what he believes is superior painting. George does not respond to the issue but criticises her mother's grammatical inaccuracies leading to a conversation in which Carol holds the position that 'language is a living growing changing organism [...] which follows its own rules and alters them as it likes' (pp. 195–6) and George is accused of pedantry for wanting to uphold its rules. Carol, on the side of flux, appears to be on the approved side of the binary; focus on grammar is an evasion by George of the serious topic of conversation which is at first about value and reward, then about binaries themselves. She demands more information:

> Is it happening now or in the past? George says. Is the artist a woman or a man?
>
> Do either of those things matter? her mother says.
>
> Does either, George says. Either being singular.
>
> Mea maxima, her mother says.

> I just don't get why you won't commit, ever, George says. (p. 193)

Before this remembered conversation, at the very start of the 'Camera' section, George reveals that grief has dissolved her grammatical rigidity, her pedantry:

> At least they've used an apostrophe, the George from before her mother died says.
>
> I do not give a fuck about whether some site on the internet attends to grammatical correctness, the George from after says. (p. 191)

The comic incongruity between grammar and death, the visual surface of language and its content, is part of an enquiry here into the differences between visual and verbal interpretation. But grammatical pedantry also signifies an interest in fixity and fluidity that goes to the heart of the novel's interest in gender. George's mother's death has thrown her into chaos – an unwelcome form of fluidity – but there is a subtext to the earlier conversation about art and value indicated not just by the strength of the closing plea but by the fact that when her mother describes language as a living 'organism', the image of a book that she used to own 'How to Achieve Good Orgasm' (another grammatically inelegant phrase) is spontaneously evoked for George. George is curious, perhaps prurient, about her mother's friendship with a woman called Lisa Goliard. Her desire for her mother to 'commit' seems freighted with much more weight than a request for grammatical accuracy, just as the strictures of binary linguistic constructions impose cruelly on those who wish to live outside of them.

The tension between fixity and fluidity is part of the novel's interest in structures of looking, in art and sexuality, and in the interaction of its two historical periods. In the storyworld, George's desire for things to be known and fixed is presented as symptomatic of her age (adolescence) and the age ('pics or it didn't happen'). When she explains to her counsellor that she and her mother wondered if her mother was under surveillance, if Lisa Goliard was a spy, Mrs Rock explains the etymology of the word 'mystery'; it 'originally meant a closing, of the mouth or the eyes. It meant an agreement or an understanding that something would not be disclosed' (p. 258). George ponders this idea of things remaining unrevealed, unmarked. During the visit to Ferrara, and thus after the conversation above, George confesses to her mother that she once replied to Lisa as her mother on her mother's mobile phone, telling Lisa that she was too busy with her family to see her. Carol is highly entertained by this, and explains that:

> even though I suspected I'd been played [by Goliard], there was something. It was true, and it was passionate. It was unsaid. It was left to the understanding. To the imagination. [...] And most of all, my darling. The being seen. The being watched. It makes life very, well I don't know. Pert. [...] Seeing and being seen, Georgie, is very rarely simple, her mother says. (pp. 308–9)

Here being seen, witnessed, is pleasurable precisely because it was not explained, spelt out and thus fixed in language. It was complex rather than simple. Carol's declaration calls to mind Phelan's 'Memory. Sight. Love. All require a witness, imagined or real' and in doing so provides context for George's behaviour in scenes which are presented earlier in the narrative but which occur later chronologically.[14] Carol has explained her own pleasure in the relationship with Goliard, but the conversation seems strangely neglectful of George's feelings. Carol describes her gratification in being watched as feeling 'permitted [...] Like I was *being allowed*' (p. 310). She does not spell out the ways in which she is being permitted but the most obvious seem to be as a sexual being, experiencing same-sex desire (she and Lisa share a passionate kiss) and as a political activist (the Subverts are anonymous). She is being seen as she wishes to be seen; her secret identities are being witnessed, and Lisa Goliard is the spectator who provides 'self-authority, assurance, presence' in the story that Carol tells.

The erotic division of labour between the subject and the object of the gaze is linked to power here by associations with surveillance and subversion, but the link is also visible on the surface of language. At the level of referential content, the narrative presents issues of surface and depth, the glamorous secrets of having a lover and being an activist, which are independent of Carol's known public identities of mother and wife. At this level, the relation between truth and lies also has the temporal dimension, since secrets belong to the life of adults, the adulthood that George approaches. In the service of this theme, after Carol's death, George's father is angry when she talks about the possible surveillance, believing it to be an adolescent fantasy of Carol's '*to distract her from her life and how do you think that makes me feel, George?*' (p. 283). Lisa Goliard may not have been a spy, but she does not seem to be the artist she said she was. And this is what can also be seen on the surface of language: as George tells us, she is a liar, and the word 'liar' is embedded in her name, nested graphically in the word 'God', the symbol of ultimate surveillance. That her name contains the word 'liar' indicates her role in the text as a signifier of uncertainty, the unsettling power of that which cannot be known. And yet it is the combination between what cannot be seen or known and godlike omniscience that seems to confer bothness on Lisa. In contrast to her husband's slight, Carol's failure to commit seems more an expression of maturity; her response to George's assertion that 'It can't be both. It must be one or the other', the question 'Why must it?' (p. 194) is a refusal to be fixed into a single identity.

At every stage, the linguistic surface, both its visual surface and its grammatical conventions, co-operate in this way with the enquiry into what can be seen and what is unmarked. Smith's stub of a title, intrigues in its incompletion: how to be both what and what? That the 'b' of 'both' is not capitalised suggests that 'both' is functioning here as an adverb or adjective rather than a pronoun, but even if read as a pronoun, of course, there is no sense of what two elements it is standing for. This is one of the uses of the pronoun in everyday discourse; to stand in for something the speaker does not want to spell out or pin down but instead imply – 'he's one of *those*', 'do you think they're doing *it*?' – especially with reference to the unknown, titillating or taboo of sexuality. As a pronoun on its own 'both', paradoxically, suggests twoness, duality, two things perhaps two people, something impossible. The grammatical incompletion of Smith's title embodies *and* emphasises the impossibility of its proposition, but it also invests its two missing, invisible words with a considerable power. It achieves and retains the power of the unmarked.

IV. Invisibility and blindness

The value of 'bothness', for this novel, is in the becoming simultaneous of things separated in time, which is the very essence of del Cossa's frieze of the seasons, and yet this becoming space of time is never quite separable from, because it is the structure of, gender ambiguity: as a representation of all twelve months in one frame, the frieze is an emblem of an impossible and unsettling spatial co-presence, or spatialisation of time. Carol's love of bothness, of ambiguity, is the key to her love of the Ferrara frieze, the first thing that has made her happy since her friendship with Lisa Goliard mysteriously (to her) ended. In it she finds 'constant sexual and gender ambiguities running through the whole work' leading to her claim '[o]n this alone I could make a reasonably witty argument for its originator being female, if I had to' (p. 297). Here maleness is certainty, being female is ambiguous unfixed Otherness. In that moment, George scoffs at the lingering influence of her mother's art history and women's studies degrees, but there is a case to be made for George as author of 'Eyes' – the anachronisms, the misspellings of Franchesco – enacting her mother's beliefs, telling the story of del Cossa as a woman not a man. In adolescence, George is left without a mother; her actions and behaviour instead are shaped by recent memories of Carol and the profound questions she asked. This happens perhaps in her choice of school project but also happens in terms of George's own sexuality and identity as female.

Phelan's assertion that 'the desire to be seen is also activated by looking at inanimate art' is given credence throughout the novel, here in Carol's delight.[15] The memory of her pleasure in 'being seen', which was at least partly about sexual desire and identity as a sexual being, as well as her death, provides a context for George's subsequent behaviour. These issues are at their most visible in those sections of the novel that deal openly with pornographic representation. Deciding that not having had sex and not having seen any porn were 'like doubly being a virgin' (p. 217) – another doubling – George takes her iPad into the garden, away from potential discovery by her younger brother, and watches some. The films that intrigue her are described in the diegesis through the focalisation of her innocent curiosity. The first film features a younger woman led by an older woman, both stylishly dressed, into what looks to George 'like a gym' but which we recognise as an S&M dungeon. The older woman drops a blinding liquid into the eyes of the younger woman so that she cannot see what is to be done to her (she is the passive object of the gaze, the acted upon rather than active as conventional pornography prescribes); George sees only flashes of 'extreme-looking moments' since the full film is only available upon subscription (flashes are all that a young person knows about sex). The passage is full of sight metaphors, reflecting the structures of looking and watching that characterise pornography. But a slip in time from 'Eyes' into 'Camera' provides insight into what is happening to George as she views. In 'Eyes', Franchesco, as a ghost, watches George watching pornography and states 'this is a girl with a very strong eye' (p. 67). Franchesco means that the scene is extreme or disturbing, but the phrase has the homophone of 'I': this is a girl with a very strong I, a strong sense of self? Grief and adolescence mean that George does not seem to have a strong sense of self, but she is engaged in a process of self-discovery as to what it means to be female, and a sexual being, in western society. When George asks whether the blinding of the young woman in the film is permanent, she calls to mind a Shakespearean plot, other elements of which might be the cross-dressing of 'Eyes', or the gender confusion when Franchesco's ghost realises of George 'this boy is a girl' (p. 65). The scene refers to St Lucy, of whom it is said variously that her eyes were gouged out and she was raped in a brothel as punishment for refusing to burn a sacrifice, or that she removed her own eyes to avoid the gaze of a suitor.

The film thus draws together many of the novel's tropes and allusions. But whilst it seems only to intrigue George, another profoundly disturbs her, and seems to do so through the identification of eye and I that women experience in watching conventional pornography. As Phelan describes, '[t]he process of self-identity is a leap into a narrative that employs seeing as a way of knowing' but '[t]aking the world in is a process of loss: learning to see is training careful blindness'.[16] The 'careful blindness' has yet to be learnt by George; the one which will shield her from the pain of identifying with the victimised female. The third film that is described in the diegesis concerns a girl who 'looked about twelve' (p. 221). George's naivety seems to allow her to hope that the girl 'must have been sixteen because of legality' (p. 221) but the film disturbs her even so. The girl looks drugged and is discomforted; her abuser is an older man. Once seen, George cannot unsee the girl:

> Afterwards when George tried to watch any more of this kind of sexual film that girl was there waiting under them all.

More. George found that the girl was there too, pale and pained with her shut eyes and her open o of a mouth, under the surface of the next TV show she watched on catch-up.

She was there under the YouTube videos of Vampire Weekend and the puppy falling off the sofa and the cat sitting on the hoover.... (p. 221)

Thus haunted by the film, George decides to watch it every day to bear witness to its horrors and the terrible things that happen everywhere on a daily basis. She wants her actions to form a kind of penance for the girl. This sweet childish gesture begins while her mother is still alive, but George is caught watching the film by her father after Carol has died. It is significant that this is one of the very few scenes in the novel in which her father appears; the next is also a monitoring of her sexuality. His exasperation, anxiety, grief perhaps lead him to make a very poor attempt to console, one which fails to convince and illuminates the degree of loss that George has suffered in her mother dying. He says of the abused girl '[s]he was probably very well paid for it' (p. 224), unfortunately aligning himself with the wrong side of the binary which pits male power and capital against the vulnerable female slave. George struggles to explain to her father why her viewing is different but he responds that these repeated viewings online will only serve to raise the film's popularity, raising it to the top of whatever search led George to it in the first place. In the world, George's actions which were forged with the best intentions will encourage replication of the crime. But her repeated viewings of the film must be read as the response to and attempt to resolve a trauma.

These questions of vision and power are explored, characteristically for Smith, in associative and tropological ways, in a way that is never quite separable from her concerns with the visual surface of language itself. But the enquiry is also never distant from the ideas that it encodes so suggestively, or from the more discursive expression of critical and philosophical debates. In remembering the trip to Ferrara, George recalls one such debate which irritated her at the time. Carol told George that after a flood had damaged the frieze, restorers discovered pictures below that were different to those on the surface. Asking which came first, the frieze or the sketches underneath, Carol muses:

But the first thing we see [...] and most times the only thing we see, is the one on the surface. So does that mean it comes first after all? And does that mean the other picture, if we don't know about it, may as well not exist? (p. 289)

Carol is asking her daughter to think about history; her conversation turns to the executions that happened during the First World War in the square in which they sit. Poignantly, as it turns out, she is asking for remembrance. But the question has clear parallels with concerns about visibility and identity.

('Memory. Sight. Love. All require a witness, imagined or real'). In repeatedly watching the rape of the girl, George is refusing to forget her and the many victims like her. For George, the internet parallels Carol's frieze; she cannot unsee what is underneath, the girl and her trauma, when looking at the trivial entertainments on the surface. She sees both. Her mother asked her to bear witness and she does. In 'Camera', there are several scenes which draw attention to the simultaneities and repetitions afforded by the internet; in one, George watches a programme about the Flying Scotsman on two screens, from half-way through on TV and from the start on her laptop. What can be seen on screens now, the simultaneous, endless transmissions of many pasts is the visual representation of memory. The image here is partly that of the multiplicity that comes from simultaneity, but it also evokes the basic time structure that runs through the novel and my argument, of uncertainty in relation to the before and after. And many of the novel's details work in the service of this same ambiguity or temporal inversion, often in ways that return us to its central concern with being both man and woman, such as the performance of *As You Like It*, that Shakespearean tract on gender ambiguity, that George watches in the wrong order, first from middle to end, then from start to middle, so superimposing the technological issues of recording once again onto the Shakespearean motif, and in the process enacting the duality of its own form as a novel.

Sometimes these interests in visibility and abuse read like straightforward warnings about the dangers of recording and surveillance in the digital age. It is not only grief, one form of love, which unmoors George. She falls in love with Helena Fisker, a bold girl at school, who saves her from one of the many humiliating forms of bullying enabled by technology. The year 9 girls loiter in the school toilets to record the sound of other girls urinating, on their phones. These sound files are then distributed to boys whose disgust is particularly strong for those who are deemed to wee loudly. The surveillance of female bodies happens everywhere. George was being filmed coming out of a cubicle when Helena snatched the phone from the filmer and dropped it into the toilet. George wonders if the phone's memory has survived, because if so 'it meant there was a recording of her somewhere and in it she was looking straight over their heads into the eyes of Helena Fisker' (p. 264). Once they are friends, as a further test of their compatibility, George tentatively asks Helena if she believes that her mother might have been under surveillance. They are in Carol's study at the time. As an affirmative answer, Helena lists the kinds of monitoring that we are all under, concluding as a sexual overture that she would monitor George. (Through her watchfulness, she has already saved George from the unwelcome surveillance in the school toilets). In this conversation and in George's pondering about the survival of the phone's memory, seeing is for the girls, as for Carol, a declaration of sexual desire and of identity. Mr Cook has been standing at the door, has overheard this conversation (again monitoring her sexuality), and rather than address what really concerns him (the girls' relationship) requests that they leave Carol's study, metaphorically amounting to an expulsion from her mother's space, perhaps her mother's sexuality. Nevertheless, as a witness, he is the spectator who determines it.

V. Unmarked flashes of the future

Towards the end of her part of the novel, 'Camera', George's pedantry returns; she corrects Helena's grammar. It is not the case that a realisation of her own homosexuality leads her to happily embrace 'they' and grammatical fluidity. As for Maggie Nelson in the memoir of her relationship with fluidly gendered Harry Dodge, instead, love is asserted through rigour. Remembering feminist study, reading Irigaray, a theorist whose analysis of the 'sex which is not one' seems germane to a theory of bothness, Nelson expounds:

> It's easy to get juiced up about a concept like plurality or multiplicity and start complimenting everything as such. [Eve Kosovsky] Sedgwick was impatient with that kind of sloppy praise. Instead, she spent a lot of time talking and writing about that which is more than one, and more than two, but less than infinity.
>
> This finitude is important. It makes possible the great mantra, the great invitation, of Sedgwick's work, which is to 'pluralize and specify.' (Barthes: 'One must pluralize, refine, continuously.') This is an activity that demands an attentiveness – a relentlessness, even – whose very rigor tips it into ardor.[17]

Towards the end of 'Camera', George cycles to the outskirts of Cambridge, by Addenbrooke's Hospital where her mother died, and along the DNA cycle path which is marked at each end by a sculpture of the double helix. The path is marked by 10,257 coloured rectangles which stand for the components of the human gene. She cycles from one sculpture to the other, precisely the length of the gene, and from that distance photographs the sculpture at the other end. She sends the image to Helena. To George, the spring-like twist of the sculpture represents that which cannot be repressed, a shout which is 'real' history. The helix's double twist is a description of the two parts of the novel. The scene, like the novel itself, is richly overdetermined. The cycle path and the sculptures magnify with the precision that which cannot be seen, a form of knowledge which is recently known. It speaks of scientific precision but to George signifies an emotion, the revolutionary spirit of 'real' history. Within the novel, the scene literalises the metaphor of distance with which George has needed to travel to gain perspective. She first saw what looked like a helix from the window of a train, then cycles out of Cambridge to see that it really is a sculpture of the form, then cycles to the end of the path to photograph it and send it to Helena, the girl who represents her future, or the possibility of future that grief denied her to this moment:

> That's when she sensed, like something blurred and moving glimpsed through a partition whose glass is clouded, both that love was coming for her and the nothing she could do about it.
> The cloud of unknowing, her mother said in her ear.
> Meets the cloud of knowing, George thought back. (p. 358)

The last few pages of 'Camera' contain flashes of future scenes. In one, George corrects Mrs Rock's grammar from 'their' to 'his or her', in another George sits in front of del Cossa's portrait of St Vincent Ferrer in the National Gallery, London, which she has taken to doing daily. Another woman looks at the painting and George realises it is Lisa Goliard. In the final scene, which has not happened yet – 'none of the above has happened' (p. 371) – she has followed Goliard home and sits on the wall opposite her house watching and photographing.

Another kind of 'unmarked' presents itself in this scene in the form of that which cannot be known: not the invisible or the socially excluded, but that which lies ahead, in the realm of the not yet. I want to conclude by considering this notion – of the unmarked as an invisible future – as a possible way in which feminism and queer narratology might reattach the invisible to power, in the form of possibility. This is a prominent theme in Smith's earlier novels, most notably *There but for the*, which consistently images the future as a blocked telescope, or that which cannot be seen from any distance.[18] Like Warhol's very productive narratological concept of the unnarrated, the unmarked has a potential to speak of narrative gaps and blindnesses, and so connect narrative to representational visibility, but as Phelan makes clear, to yoke power to the visible is somehow to relinquish a different power that resides in the invisible.[19] Both the 'unmarked' and the 'unnarrated' display the tendency that I ascribed to the image in the opening section, to point both forwards and backwards. Hence, the 'unnarrated' can be conceived as a gap in what was represented in retrospect in an existing storyworld, but equally as a narrative future, or as that which lies ahead, like the missing words of Smith's title. This is what might help us to link the unmarked to political possibility, or blindness to power, since it is what does not already exist in representation that most clearly defines the realm of possibility, and the opportunity to usher in a future as other and not as the same, or new possibilities which do not exist in representations of what already exists. This is, unquestionably what is at stake in Smith's novel, not only in its engagement with history, or in its flashes of the narrative future, but in its palpable, graphic interests in formal innovation itself. The political significance of this kind of formal invention might then be something like a retort to *Miss Representation*'s slogan 'you can't be what you can't see', and which I take to be the core of Phelan's argument (a retort that comes in advance): that you cannot always see what you can be.

Notes

1. Peggy Phelan, *Unmarked: The Politics of Performance* (London and New York: Routledge, 1993), p. 10.
2. Attributed to Marian Wright Edelman in Jennifer Sibel Newsom, dir. *Miss Representation* (2017). http://therepresentationproject.org/film/miss-representation [Date accessed: 4 July 2017].
3. See, for example, https://www.theguardian.com/news/2015/feb/26/pics-or-it-didnt-happen-mantra-instagram-era-facebook-twitter [Date accessed: 4 July 2017].
4. See Jacques Derrida, *Archive Fever: A Freudian Impression*, trans. Eric Prenowitz (Chicago, IL: University of Chicago Press, 1995) and Bernard Stiegler, 'Memory', in Mark B.N. Hansen and W.J.T. Mitchell (eds.), *Critical Terms for Media Studies* (Chicago, IL: University of Chicago Press, 2010), pp. 64–87.
5. Paul Laity, 'Interview with Maggie Nelson', *The Guardian*, 2 April 2016. https://www.theguardian.com/books/2016/apr/02/books-interview-maggie-nelson-genders [Date accessed: 4 July 2017].
6. Jacqueline Rose, 'Who Do You Think You Are?', *London Review of Books*, 9.38 (2016), p. 6.
7. Robyn Warhol, 'The Look, the Body, and the Heroine of *Persuasion*: A Feminist Narratological View of Jane Austen', in Kathy Mezei (ed.), *Ambiguous Discourse: Feminist Narratology and British Women Writers* (Chapel Hill and London: University of North Carolina Press, 1996), pp. 21–39 (p. 25).
8. Ibid.
9. Susan S. Lanser, 'Toward (a Queerer and) More (Feminist) Narratology', in Robyn Warhol and Susan S. Lanser (eds.), *Narrative Theory Unbound: Queer and Feminist Interventions* (Columbus: The Ohio State University Press, 2015), pp. 23–42 (p. 30).
10. Ibid.
11. See Martin Hägglund, *Dying for Time: Proust, Woolf, Nabokov* (Cambridge, MA: Harvard University Press, 2012).
12. Ali Smith, *How to Be Both* (London: Penguin, 2014). Page numbers are for an edition of the novel which begins with 'Eyes'.
13. If you have an e-book version, a statement alerts you to the two forms of the paper book and invites you to make your own mind up about whether to read 'Camera' or 'Eyes' first, which is a responsibility and thus a different experience entirely.
14. Phelan, *Unmarked*, p. 5.
15. Ibid., p. 4.
16. Ibid., pp. 4, 14.
17. Maggie Nelson, *The Argonauts* (London: Melville House UK, 2016), pp. 77–8.
18. Ali Smith, *There But For The* (London: Hamish Hamilton, 2011).
19. Robyn R. Warhol, 'Neonarrative; or, How to Render the Unnarratable in Realist Fiction and Contemporary Film', in James Phelan and Peer J. Rabinowitz (eds.), *A Companion to Narrative Theory* (Oxford: Blackwell, 2005), pp. 220–31.

Disclosure statement

No potential conflict of interest was reported by the author.

The unspeakable, the unnarratable, and the repudiation of epiphany in 'Recitatif': a collaboration between linguistic and literary feminist narratologies

Robyn Warhol and Amy Shuman

ABSTRACT
The authors bring together feminist-narratological methodologies from literary studies and linguistic anthropology in a reading of Toni Morrison's short story, 'Recitatif'. Both authors self-identify as 'feminist narratologists', but their two fields seldom interact. They ask what insights their combined approaches bring to interpreting this radically ambiguous fictional text that distinguishes two characters as being 'black' and 'white' without establishing which is which. Instead, race and class are discursively constructed out of perceived difference and affiliation. Pursuing the linguistic discourse analyst's interest in 'the unspeakable' and the literary critic's formulation of 'the unnarratable', rather than ask 'Who is speaking?' the authors consider who cannot or will not speak, especially Maggie, the disabled character whom the narrator assumes is incapable of speech. Morrison's story substitutes shame for the sympathy that readers might ordinarily experience in reading progressive narratives about otherness. Instead of ending on a 'relatable' epiphany, 'Recitatif' presents two protagonists ashamed of their failure to read disability (or even to have understood that disability is neither self-evident nor transparent), just as the story's readers are shamed for their assumption that race shouldn't need to be read, because – as the narrator's silences imply – it supposedly goes without saying.

For a long time, both of us (Amy, a linguistic anthropologist and folklorist; and Robyn, a literary and pop-culture theorist and critic) have called ourselves 'feminist narratologists'. We both study narrative structures with an eye toward the differences that gender, race, class, disability, sexuality, and nationality make. We both have spent decades arguing that structuralist, formalist and cognitive narrative theories exclude the experiences and the texts of too many readers, speakers, and writers when they universalise the 'human', and we have both developed methods for making narratologies more inclusive and more culturally specific. Grounding her work in discourse analysis, Amy's interactive, ethnographic approach attends to how real-world speakers navigate their responsibilities to each other. Robyn's approach does not focus on the language or positionality of actual people, but examines the ways narratives produce the illusion of characters' interiorities and use narrators to manage readerly affect. Though the 'I' and 'you' in Amy's texts have real-world referents and those in Robyn's (usually) do not, we are both interested in the work our texts do in the world, coming together in our analyses of the ways stigma and oppression are managed in narrative discourse. And yet, few people inside academia would recognise us as belonging to the same field.

When we two drew up the reading list for a Project Narrative Summer Institute on queer and feminist narratology at the Ohio State University in 2014, we were struck by how few foundational readings we shared in common. If we go all the way back to the pre-feminist roots of narratology, we find a common heritage that includes Vladimir Propp, Claude Levi-Strauss, and Ferdinand de Saussure, structuralists whose work in folklore, anthropology, and linguistics formed much of the theoretical grounding for the narratology that A. J. Greimas, Gérard Genette, Gerald Prince, Mieke Bal and others were to pioneer. In its origins during the 1980s, literary feminist narratology would not have got off the ground without the influence of such linguists as J. L. Austin and Roman Jakobson, whose theories of performativity and referentiality partly enabled the original feminist critique of structuralist narratology's blindness to the differences that gender makes. In her ground-breaking 1986 essay, 'Toward a Feminist Narratology', Susan S. Lanser cited Levi-Strauss as well as Robin Lakoff's 'Language and Woman's Place' (1973) and Sally McConnell-Ginet's *Women and Language in Literature and Society* (1980), sources that are essential to the anthropological-linguistic approach.[1] At some point after feminism and narratology got introduced, however, the literary and the linguistic-anthropological approaches stopped interacting with each other. Lanser is a titan in both our sub-disciplines, having written not just the most wide-ranging and influential works in Robyn's field, but also some staples of Amy's, including 'Burning Dinners: Feminist Subversions of Domesticity' (1992).[2] And yet, Robyn – for whom Lanser is a primary influence and valued collaborator – had never read 'Burning Dinners', nor even heard of it before Amy told her how important it is to feminist folklorists. The only scholar we could think of who has consistently crossed between our two fields is Ruth Page, whose *Literary and Linguistic Approaches to Feminist Narratology* (2006) took a step toward starting a conversation that has never quite taken hold.[3] What would happen if literary and linguistic feminist narratology were to enter into a truly interdisciplinary collaboration? What could a combined feminist narrative-theoretical approach add to the insights that our seemingly separate disciplines have already achieved? We decided to find out by bringing our joined methodologies to bear on a notoriously inscrutable piece of narrative fiction, Toni Morrison's 'Recitatif' (1983).[4]

As others who have written about Morrison's only short story have observed, 'recitative' is a form of musical declamation used in oratorios and operas to convey any narration or dialogue that occurs in between arias and choruses. A type of sung speech, recitative is minimally musical, employing rhythm and pitch but no melody for the solo voice and no vocal harmonies to join it. Formally, recitative is more like chant than it is like song, and functionally it is an expository interlude of neutral affect, a breathing space in between the emotive intensity of the choruses and arias. The implications of calling a short story 'Recitatif' are open to interpretation, but we want to emphasise the title's reference to the impossibility of speaking. When a narrator or character in an opera or oratorio has something to tell, there can be no talking, only recitative. To us, this implies that the story's situation of enunciation – a character-narrator recounting events of her own life to an uncharacterised narratee – is to be understood as something different from ordinary speaking. Our project in this essay is to outline what that difference entails.

Morrison has described 'Recitatif' as 'an experiment in the removal of all racial codes from a narrative about two characters of different races for whom racial identity is crucial'.[5] Morrison's story tells of two girls assigned to be roommates in an orphanage, Twyla and Roberta, who encounter each other at intervals throughout their lives. Twyla, the narrator, implies at the outset that one of them is black and the other is white, but she never establishes which one is which, and the girls' respective racial identities are never referenced in dialogue between the two of them or with other characters. The result is a narrative that refuses to rest on assumptions about what it means to be black or to be white, while focusing on the growing difference between Twyla's and Roberta's social class standing. As bloggers and commentators on the internet often point out, readers' first impulse is often to assume that Twyla, the lower-class character, is black and Roberta, the upper-class character, is white. The story contains enough contradictory bits of evidence to call that automatic equivalence between race and social status into question, and it can be difficult or even impossible to establish whether the meaning of those bits of evidence inheres in assumptions about race or class or a conflation of the two. The consensus about 'Recitatif' is that it remains radically ambiguous in its presentation of race in order to force readers to re-think their own unquestioned assumptions about what constitutes racial identity.[6]

While we agree that the reader of 'Recitatif' must confront her own inclinations toward racial profiling, we think the question of who is black and who is white is secondary to the story's even more important point: race does not inhere in any person, but is discursively constructed out of perceived difference and affiliation. At every turn, Twyla experiences the racial divide between herself and Roberta – 'a girl from a whole other race' – in terms of otherness. Morrison is careful to keep the signifiers of that otherness ambiguous, so that they refer only equivocally to blackness or to whiteness, if they seem to be referential at all. While some readers take this to mean that class has become more important than race as a dividing social force, the point is not that race no longer signifies in a supposedly post-racial society, but that the signifiers of race are arbitrary and slippery even though, as we have quoted Morrison as saying, 'racial identity is crucial'. In 'Recitatif', racial identity is both obvious and important to Twyla and Roberta as well as to the characters around them, all of whom can see what Twyla will not say: which girl is black and which is white. In prose narrative as opposed to, say, film or graphic novels, race is invisible and can only be indicated with discursive markers. If the narrator cannot or will not tell – because to her and to her narratee it's too obvious, it goes without saying – that is, if she is performing a recitative rather than speaking in the ordinary way, then the markers Morrison gives us can indicate only racial difference, rather than race itself.

If the story's title points to Twyla's ability metaphorically to perform a recitative, it also draws attention to the themes of what can and cannot be told, who can and cannot speak. In what follows, we will examine the formal manifestations of what can't or won't be told in 'Recitatif' before moving into the thematic implications of those formal features. We are interested in what the narrator will not (or does not need to) speak about, and also in who can speak, who cannot speak, and precisely how the characters do speak to one another. What Amy calls 'the unspeakable', Robyn calls 'the unnarratable'.[7] Neither category is defined by content alone; both are descriptors of the strategies people or narrators use when refusing to put something into words, whether for secrecy, misdirection, denial, perversity, literary convention, or some other purpose. Both of our approaches continually ask 'Who is speaking? To whom? For what purpose?'. Reading 'Recitatif' together, we arrived at questions about who is *not* speaking – a narrator who won't tell what the reader wants to know, a character who can't say what she might have wanted to express. The presence of a mute character, Maggie, foregrounds Morrison's awareness of the metaphorical way feminists have used the idea of 'finding one's voice' or 'speaking out'. The story reminds us that 'Can the subaltern speak?' does not mean 'Is the subordinated person capable of vocalizing words?'.[8] By bringing Maggie's disability into the story, Morrison returns the question of 'who can speak' from the realms that discourse analysts and literary narratologists generally frequent to the realm of the body, which turns out to be as unreadable and indeterminate as the text itself.

What happened when we combined Amy's interactive, ethnographic method with Robyn's literary, structural analysis was that we perceived an underlying logic in the story, something we think neither of us was likely to have discovered with our own approach alone. Because of the lack of descriptive information (a feature of many short stories), the insufficient recounting of backstory or events, and the frequent absence of discourse markers (such as 'I said', 'she said'), we might each have been able to describe the story's narrative strategies but we could not get to a satisfactory interpretation. Reading as two kinds of feminist narratologists together, one looking for indexicality and the other for narrative exposition, we discovered affect (the two protagonists' liking each other, raging at each other, and sharing shame with each other and with the reader) instead. We concluded that Morrison's story substitutes shame for the sympathy readers are ordinarily supposed to experience in reading progressive narratives about otherness. Instead of ending on a 'relatable' epiphany, 'Recitatif' presents two protagonists ashamed of their failure to read disability (or even to have understood that disability is neither self-evident nor transparent), just as the story's readers ought to feel ashamed of their assumption that race shouldn't need to be read, because – as the narrator's silences imply – it supposedly goes without saying.

Experiments in the unnarratable

In a 1993 *Paris Review* interview, Toni Morrison has explained how William Faulkner's *Absalom, Absalom!* (1936) inspired her to experiment with the representation of race in 'Recitatif'.[9] 'What is exciting about American literature', she says, is 'how writers say things under, beneath, and around their stories'. To 'say' things in this way is *not* to articulate them at any level of the narrative discourse. As Morrison sees it, Faulkner 'spends the entire book tracing race and you can't find it. No one can see it, even the character who *is* Black can't see it'. Morrison attributes this effect to 'the *structure* of the book', made up of 'all the moments of withheld, partial, or dis-information, when a racial fact or clue *sort* of comes out but doesn't quite arrive' (emphasis in original). That structure ensures that 'as a reader you have been forced to hunt for a drop of black blood that means everything and nothing', so that you must face the arbitrariness of the category 'Black' as well as the ambiguity of its significance. In *Absalom*, she concludes, 'the structure is the argument' and the argument is 'the insanity of racism'.[10]

Authors who 'say things under, beneath, and around their stories' are trafficking in what literary feminist narratology would call the *unnarratable*, that which in a given historical moment and a particular genre cannot (the supranarratable), need not (the subnarratable), or should not (the antinarratable) be told.[11] Morrison's interest in the unnarratable runs throughout all her writing, from her making nonsense out of the 'Dick and Jane' stories in

The Bluest Eye; to the inexplicable return of the dead daughter in *Beloved*; to the constant, unspoken presence of African-Americans in white-authored American fiction that Morrison names in 'Playing in the Dark'. In American fiction race is usually specified and always coded: this character is black, that one is white, and once the narration has established those conditions, the authorial audience attaches to each character all the connotations and stereotypes those racial terms signify in US culture. Race, in American literary tradition, is subnarratable: what blackness or whiteness means doesn't need to be told because it is supposed to be taken for granted – it goes without saying.

In 'Recitatif', Morrison exposes the subnarratable status of race not by narrating it more explicitly than literary convention would dictate, as some authors might do, but by eliminating all signs that would ordinarily indicate received meanings (black, white; nappy hair, stringy hair; ebony skin, ivory skin, etc.). As we have noted, one of the effects of this is to make actual readers aware of how unconsciously they typically rely on clichés and stereotypes to understand who a character is and how that character relates to others. Once all those markers of race are absent from a story where racial difference is the main complication producing the plot, the reader is left with a consciousness of her own racism, as well as a text so irreducibly ambiguous as to reward repeated re-reading with further perplexity. Though Morrison (in the *Paris Review* interview) described the experiment as 'a lark', treating it as a tour-de-force of form, we want to emphasise the political work that the text is doing when it engages readers in this way.

When we say 'the reader', we mean the actual person who holds the book and reads, a person whose political and ethical engagements have real-world consequences. When the reader moves from reading to action – even if that action is only to accept a new insight about her own racist assumptions, whatever her personal racial identity may be – the story is accomplishing political work in the real world. The reader is not to be conflated, however, with the narratee, the virtual figure to whom the narrator is speaking in a story structured like 'Recitatif'. Identifying the characteristics of a narratee is an exercise in Bakhtinian dialogics, that is, in analysing the knowledge, attitudes, assumptions, and beliefs the narrator is implicitly answering as she tells the story. The narratee of 'Recitatif' appears to occupy no particular racial position. Twyla as narrator is speaking to someone who evidently shares her own prejudices about the 'other' race, someone who understands Twyla's class position and sympathises with her social politics, especially as they contrast with Roberta's. Twyla does not demonstrate a need to explain or defend her own attitudes to her narratee. But whether that addressee is black or white is as indeterminate as what race the characters are meant to be. As our analysis will show, this racially ambiguous address directs the story to all actual readers who harbour racist attitudes, no matter how unconsciously. Ambiguity might sometimes serve as a postmodernist dodge to avoid taking a political stand, but in Morrison's text ambiguity is at the heart of the story's activism against 'the insanity of racism'.

The formal and structural production of ambiguity

When the unnarratable surfaces in texts through indicators of what can't, need not, or shouldn't be told, ambiguity is the inevitable result.[12] Katharine Young's ethnographic work on conversational narrative provides a useful list of the formal producers of ambiguity in her study of indirection, a form of interactive narrative communication that is indeterminate, if not ambiguous. She writes,

> Indirection is the capacity for presenting, mentioning, or alluding to matters in a roundabout way: either by touching on them obliquely, metaphorically, and unspecifically; by implication, allusion, or analogy; or by the formalization or ritualization of discourse. Indirect discourse is subtle, suggestive, or circuitous, rather than bold and direct.[13]

A linguistic-anthropological approach to narrative ambiguity primarily focuses on the conditions that produce the possibility of multiple or indeterminate interpretations, whether conditions of the text or of the interaction.[14] Further, linguistic anthropologists and others who study narrative in interaction (collected in ethnographic research) are particularly interested in how texts create and rely on shared social meanings that are often implied rather than explicitly stated.

Linguistic anthropologists identify narrative ambiguity not only in terms of missing or confusing referents but also in terms of the information provided or not provided by the structure of an utterance. For instance, in an essay revisiting his classical study of narrative structure, William Labov has shown how the phrase 'exactly the same' yields different possible interpretations.[15] Most often, for linguistic anthropologists, the question is not the presence or absence of referents but the use of short cuts (indexicalities), that signal in-group understanding and that often are the site of contested interpretations.[16]

In one of the most radically ambiguous narrative moments in 'Recitatif', Twyla reports her thoughts about Roberta's adult social position during the scene when the two women, mothers themselves now, clash over forced busing between school districts, which was a 1960s and 1970s strategy for promoting racial integration by battling the 'separate but equal' ideology of segregation. Twyla-as-narrator remarks of Roberta and her cohort, 'Everything is so easy for them. They think they own the world'. The unidentified 'them', who 'think they own the world' appears again a moment later. Addressing her sympathetic narratee, narrator-Twyla says of the protestors on the opposing side, 'Who do they think they are? Swarming all over the place like they own it'. Neither utterance tells us who 'them' is, enough to create ambiguity on the level of reference. But for a linguistic anthropologist, the structure of the exchange provides an additional level of ambiguity by affording the possibility of a general, unspecified, and therefore indeterminate statement. 'Who do they think they are?' refers to a general 'they' rather than to a particular person. Similarly, 'like they own it' doesn't refer to a specific owner but rather to the more general issue of who is entitled to be an owner. The challenge to entitlement to ownership can be brought from several perspectives, including the lower-class person challenging the entitlement of the powerful and the wealthy person challenging a person deemed insubordinate, or the black person resenting white privilege and the white person resenting the inroads gradually being gained by affirmative action. Morrison cleverly deploys not only the lack of racial reference to 'them', but also the ambiguity of a structural phrase that is open to multiple users from different class and racial positions and that means something completely different, depending on who is speaking.

Twyla's narration in 'Recitatif' navigates a constantly shifting territory between the familiar and the unfamiliar, an important component of indexicality. St. Bonny's, the state orphanage, is a shelter for displaced children, and Twyla's categorisation of the children according to their missing locations – the 'New York City Puerto Ricans and the upstate Indians' and 'even two Koreans' – emphasises their strangeness. The opening scene establishes Twyla's initial sense of otherness from her new roommate when she reports feeling 'sick to my stomach' from being 'stuck in a strange place with a girl from a whole other race'. Though the nausea born of racist disgust belongs to the child-Twyla, who focalises the scene, Roberta's unfamiliarity still lingers for the narrator-Twyla, who recalls her mother having told her about that 'whole other race' that 'they never washed their hair and they smelled funny'. In the moment of narrating, the grown-up Twyla reaffirms that difference: 'Roberta sure did. Smell funny, I mean'. Here, the shifter 'they' devolves into a specific and offensive referent, Roberta herself, while managing to remain racially ambiguous. But at St. Bonny's Twyla and Roberta become familiar to each other, setting up the contrast to their diverging lives, which later in the story will be represented not only by indeterminate racial difference and determined social class, but also by social knowledge. In their first meeting, Twyla 'liked the way [Roberta] understood things so fast', without requiring elaborate explanations for why Twyla's mother has left her at St. Bonny's. At that moment, about two pages into the story, the narrator's 'I' morphs into a 'we' that speaks for the two girls' mutual understanding and their unspoken agreement to elide the racial difference between them, even though others won't let them forget it. As narrator-Twyla says, 'It didn't matter that we looked like salt and pepper standing there and that's what the other kids called us sometimes'. From this moment until the end of the St. Bonny's sequence, when their differences once again become reified during the contrasting Easter Sunday visit of their very different mothers, Twyla's individual experiencing-'I' (as in 'I got sick to my stomach', 'I would have killed her', or 'I liked the way she understood') gives way to the Twyla + Roberta experiencing-'we' ('we were eight years old and got F's all the time', 'we weren't real orphans', or 'we should have helped [Maggie] up, I know, but we were scared').

The 'we' narrator has dissolved when Twyla and Roberta encounter each other again in the late 1960s, no longer a pair of eight-year-old girls, but young women. Twyla now works in a roadside Howard Johnson's, and Roberta is passing through with two boys on their way to see Jimi Hendrix. The two girls' former bond of mutual understanding is gone: Twyla doesn't know who Hendrix is, while Roberta professes shock at Twyla's ignorance. Choosing Hendrix is a brilliant move on Morrison's part, because of the racially ambiguous position he held as a celebrity. Acid rock was a white people's genre, but Hendrix was emphatically black, so that even though Hendrix's fans were mainly white, Roberta's enthusiasm for him and Twyla's ignorance of him tell the reader nothing definitive about their respective racial positioning. Nor does Twyla's observation that Roberta's hair 'was huge', in contrast to her own hair confined by her job's requisite hairnet. Huge hair in Hendrix's heyday, the late 1960s, might have been an outsized Afro, or it might have been a Brigitte-Bardot-style backcombed mane or a white hippie-chick's uncut, uncombed curls. What the scene does reveal is how deep the gap has become between the girls' social knowledge. Interpretation depends on shared social meanings. Later, in a moment of rapprochement, 'like sisters separated for much too long', Twyla refers to their former selves as 'Two little girls who knew what nobody else in the world knew – how not to ask questions. How to believe what had to be believed'. Knowing 'what nobody else in the world knew' codes shared social knowledge that leads to 'an understanding nod'. Their shared understanding, both here and in the opening sequence of the story, overrides the categories that otherwise divide them, whether race (which the reader does not have enough information to identify, but which the characters do know) or class (which the characters know and the reader can deduce). Refusing to rest on this moment of reconciliation, however, the story poses this shared understanding between the two friends only to contrast their mutual recognition with their inability to read the enigmatic Maggie, whose unknowability is marked as disability.

Race, class, and disability, marked and unmarked

Though Morrison deftly moves through the entire story without marking which of the two women is white and which is black, other social markers remain ambiguous in each scene of the story. In the opening sequence, the two mothers' class difference is as unspecified as their races. Twyla's mother, who has 'dumped' her daughter at the orphanage because she prefers to 'dance all night', brings only candy for Twyla to eat when she comes for the Easter visit at the orphanage. Roberta's mother, who has been too 'sick' to take care of her daughter, brings 'chicken legs and ham sandwiches and oranges and a whole box of chocolate-covered grahams'. Even though Twyla has told the matron her mother wouldn't be happy about her being assigned Roberta as a roommate, Twyla's mother grins and offers to shake hands when the two parents meet, while Roberta's mother turns away in what appears to be racist or class-based aversion, or both. Later in the story, the class difference between Roberta and Twyla becomes obvious (Roberta's husband has a white-collar job, Twyla's is blue-collar; Roberta is wearing a 'silvery evening gown and dark fur coat' when they last meet up, while Twyla is worrying about whether buying a Christmas tree would be too extravagant), but in the orphanage scenes, as we have explained, the only difference between them that signifies is race. But, as we have shown, it signifies only as difference, not as an indicator of either girl's racial identity or social class. Because Roberta's mother has provided food and Twyla's has not, we could read their class background as determined, if we assumed Twyla's mother couldn't afford to provide a substantial meal the way Roberta's mother could. But maybe Twyla's mother comes from a higher social echelon where women don't have to think about cooking for their children because someone else has been hired to do it; maybe she dances all night because she was raised to be a privileged party girl rather than a homemaker. Certainly, Twyla's mother is down on her luck, but she might not always have been. Neither mother has the economic resources at present to hire the help necessary to keep her daughter at home, but their respective class backgrounds are strictly ambiguous.

As we have said, eventually Morrison does provide clear indications of the class difference that emerges in the life trajectories of Twyla and Roberta, beginning with that first encounter after leaving the orphanage, where Twyla is waiting tables while Roberta is taking a road trip rather than working for a living. This is a key scene for drawing readers' attention to their own assumptions about the overlap between race and class. Stereotypes dictate that the more prosperous woman should be the white one and the working woman should be black, but as we have argued, other details of the scene unsettle that assumption. Morrison's super-sophisticated experiment in unearthing readers' assumptions about the overlap of race and class raises questions for us as feminist narratologists who take an intersectional approach to the discursive creation of identity positions. Why is it that disability, the category that marks Maggie (the only other named character in the story) remains undeveloped in this text? Why is disability presented as a fact rather than as a complex social construction? In other words, why does the story invite us to challenge stereotypical characterisations of race but not to challenge whether Maggie's bowleggedness or her hat are deviant? We think the answer hinges on Morrison's exposé of the supposed visibility of all identity categories. Peggy Phelan has helpfully critiqued the idea that identity can be seen:

> In conflating identity politics with visibility, cultural activists and some theorists have also assumed that 'selves' can be adequately represented within the visual or linguistic field. The 'hole in the signifier', 'the Real-impossible' which is unsayable, unseeable, and therefore resistant to representation, is ignored in the full fling into representation.[17]

We agree with Phelan's critique of the too-easy conflation of identity categories with visible and verbal signs, and the examples she cites – especially Adrian Piper's art installations – present refusals to make race identification easy that resemble those we encounter in 'Recitatif'. But as Morrison's representation of Maggie highlights, when race may be visually ambiguous, disability is supposed to show. Maggie, the elderly disabled kitchen worker who never speaks in the story, becomes the subject of the representational gaze but does not look back. Nor does Maggie participate in a reciprocal exchange with Twyla and Roberta or, by extension, with the reader. In Morrison's own terms from the interview with which we began, Maggie's identity is an example of 'a moment of withheld, partial, or dis-information', but in this case, it's not just race but also disability that '*sort of* comes out but doesn't quite arrive'.

Interestingly, in introducing Maggie, Morrison chooses to obscure one of the most visible markers of difference, skin colour, and she can do this for Maggie (as she does for all the characters in the story) because her medium is a written text.[18] Twyla describes Maggie as 'old and sandy-coloured', physical descriptors that give some substance to Maggie's appearance while remaining racially uncertain. Racial markers tend to rely on an economy of description (or of simple naming), but the other markers of difference like class require more elaboration, which the story gives us in allusions to details of visible signs like clothing. Maggie's mobility impairment is described as visible in her 'legs like parentheses', but her possible intellectual disability can only be seen in the 'really stupid little hat' she wears, and her muteness, an invisible disability. The identity categories that are not unequivocally visible are at the core of Twyla's and Roberta's uneasiness about their treatment of Maggie when they think about her later in life.

Linguistic anthropologists use the terms *marked* and *unmarked* to call attention to the default, assumed, categories that reinforce status and hierarchical relationships. Mary Bucholtz and Kira Hall define 'markedness' as a 'process whereby some social categories gain a special, default status that contrasts with the identities of other groups, which are highly recognizable'.[19] In 'Recitatif', otherwise marked racial cultural practices – including talk, religion, dress, and food – are not racially designated, though they are presented as hierarchical. Disability, in Twyla's narrative as in most of Western culture, is marked as deviant or abnormal. Maggie's disability is not named, however; instead, her deviance is produced by the taunts she endures from the 'gar girls', the bigger girls whom Roberta and Twyla fear, and eventually from the two younger girls themselves. Maggie does not speak for herself; instead, Twyla describes her by characteristics that mark her as disabled. The markers are her bowed legs, her rocking walk, and that 'really stupid little hat – a kid's hat with ear flaps'. Maggie's disability functions for Twyla and for her narratee as an uncritically marked category, like her age and her poverty, but the events of the story suggest it is the most stigmatised identity category in the context of the orphanage: St. Bonny's 'state girls', who would seem to be the lowest of the low on any social scale, place Maggie even lower by deliberately tormenting her. Though poverty is a category Maggie shares with at least some of the girls, her disability subjects her to ridicule and physical abuse, marking her as not normal and therefore not fully human. At the same time, Maggie serves as the vehicle for the shame Twyla and Roberta share in adulthood, when they think back about their experience at the orphanage. In contrast to evoking sympathy, as in the sentimental tradition where the victim is granted subjectivity and agency, the narrator-Twyla's account of her shame positions her as aware of and retrospectively willing to distance herself from the social conditions that stigmatised Maggie.[20] During the scene in the orchard, Roberta and Twyla saw themselves as having a limited choice. They dispute what happened, whether they joined the 'gar girls' in knocking Maggie down and (possibly) kicking her or they watched without intervening while Maggie suffered that abuse. Eventually, both Twyla and Roberta acknowledge to each other their complicity with the mean girls. The passage points to the political work that can be done by thoughts as well as actions.

Repudiating epiphany, owning shame

For Twyla, the recollection of the violence against Maggie brings her to an epiphany, the realisation that the 'rocking, dancing' and possibly deaf Maggie reminded Twyla of her mother, and that her own anger at her mother's inability to 'hear you if you cried in the night' made her want to see Maggie hurt. Here, Maggie serves as a metaphor, further instantiating disability as deviance. Thinking in terms of classic short story form, a reader might identify Twyla's epiphany about her mother as the main point of the story, the climax of the growing self-awareness Twyla achieves as she struggles to narrate her past. We think that Twyla's epiphany is a decoy, a misdirection Morrison uses to lure readers into a sense of impending closure that will be destabilised by the story's end.

Suppose Maggie does exist in the story merely as the vehicle for Twyla's insight. If so, disability in 'Recitatif' would be an example of what David Mitchell and Sharon Snyder have controversially called 'narrative prosthesis',[21] the ubiquity in literature of undeveloped characters with disabilities whose presence moves the action forward or motivates other characters but about whom we learn little. Such characters might speak, but they rarely gaze back. Morrison's characteristic interest in providing exactly this sort of mutual gaze for African-American girls, especially in *The Bluest Eye*, contrasts significantly with the lack of agency or character development the story accords to Maggie.[22] Instead, Maggie remains the disabled enigma who motivates Twyla and Roberta's efforts to come to terms with memories of their shared past, while the reader who can find resolution in Twyla's epiphany becomes complicit with the story's objectifying Maggie, or using her as narrative prosthesis. The story does not end on that epiphany, however, as the two women negotiate their contrasting memories of how they treated Maggie. They try to remember, but their effort remains unfinished at the end, when Roberta asks Twyla, 'Shit, shit, shit. What the hell happened to Maggie?'.

The final line of the story, this question points more to Roberta and Twyla's unfinished business with their past than to Maggie's identity or experience. For us, the question isn't so much what happened to Maggie, as whether her story can be told at all. We address this by looking at the multiple ways that the characters speak to each other, use reported speech, confessional speech, casual chit-chat, and name-calling (including *not* responding, as in the case of Maggie).[23] Each of these modes of communication implicates the reader's assessments of who is aligned with whom and with what values and social positions. In addition to Twyla's narration, the characters speak to each other through reported speech and through their picket-line posters. Each of these creates particular alignments between the characters that serve as indexes to their positions in the worlds they occupy. Fiction never fully articulates these alignments, as it both drives and leaves assessments of the positions open to the reader's interpretation. The different forms of communication point to the alignments and realignments that are central to the narrative. They also gesture to the subnarratable, or that which goes without saying.

Through alignments, Morrison shifts from sympathy to shame, from narration to dialogue and back again. Twyla and Roberta are aligned with each other against the Big Bozo and the 'gar girls' who are literally marked by their eyebrow pencil and lipstick. The two girls' alignment with each other breaks down when each of them starts aligning with others, and it is no coincidence that the shift in Twyla's discourse from the Twyla + Roberta 'we' to an 'I' and a 'she' happens at the same time that the story shifts from narration to untagged dialogue. Another of Morrison's strategies for confounding readers' desire to determine the racial identity of the two girls is the refusal to append 'she said' or 'I replied' to the dialogue. Often in this story, it is difficult to determine exactly who is speaking.

Twyla and Roberta rarely speak to each other as children, but when they do their diction shows their negotiation of their sameness and difference. On first meeting Twyla, Roberta asks, 'Is your mother sick too?', a question inviting a shared world, but Twyla explains that her mother is not sick, 'She just likes to dance all night', and Roberta appears to understand. The 'just' in Twyla's response references a different order of problem. Roberta's mother is sick, not 'just sick'. Twyla's mother 'just' likes to dance. That might mean that Twyla supposes liking to dance is a less serious problem than being sick, or perhaps that it is more normal to like to dance than to be sick. This is how inference works – the 'just' lets the reader infer that the two girls recognise Twyla's mother's dancing as a different order of problem from Roberta's mother's illness, but it does not establish what that difference signifies.

Roberta and Twyla communicate not just through dialogue, but also, later in the story, through their picket-line posters, which say something to them but are obscure to others. Rather than reveal their racial orientations toward their positions on forced busing, the posters, especially Twyla's, become increasingly personalised messages, apparently not at all related to debates about segregation. First, in response to Roberta's (unexplained) poster, reading 'MOTHERS HAVE RIGHTS TOO', Twyla waves a response saying 'HOW WOULD YOU KNOW', presumably directed to Roberta in particular and referring to their time in the orphanage. As Twyla herself says, 'My signs got crazier each day, and the women on my side decided that I was a kook. They couldn't make heads or tails out of my brilliant screaming posters'.

Of course, we, the readers, like the 'they' at the protest, are in the same position, unable to make heads or tails out of the question of what these signs mean or, for that matter, who is white and who is black. Instead, we are reminded that relationships have multiple points of reference, not only to questions of race or class but also to interpersonal interactions. As readers, we are able to follow the affective dynamics between Roberta and Twyla through narrative constructions. For example, Roberta and Twyla's disagreements are conveyed through a recognisable form of antagonism in which Twyla, asking Roberta why she is picketing, says, 'What for?' and Roberta repeats Twyla's question before answering it. Roberta says, 'What do you mean, "What for?"'. Obviously, this debate about school integration involves race, but still Morrison does not reveal which of the women is black and which white. Many readers infer that blacks or whites would be on a particular side of the issue, but Morrison destabilises those inferences. If the reader is not already willing to let go of the possibility of definitively identifying who is black and who is white, Morrison confuses us further by having the two women both say exactly the same thing to each other. Of course, it would mean something completely different depending on whether it was spoken by a black or white person:

> 'I wonder what made me think you were different'.
>
> 'I wonder what made me think you were different'.

Repetition gives us less, rather than more, information.[24]

Though their childhood dialogues with each other establish their sameness within difference, in their one direct encounter with Maggie, Twyla and Roberta address her without granting her a name:

> 'Let's call her', I said. And we did.
>
> 'Dummy! Dummy!' She never turned her head.
>
> 'Bow legs! Bow legs!' Nothing. She just rocked on, the chin straps of her baby-boy hat swaying from side to side. I think we were wrong. I think she could hear and didn't let on. And it shames me even now to think there was somebody in there after all who heard us call her those names and couldn't tell on us.

Hailed as 'Dummy' or 'Bow Legs', Maggie couldn't be an interlocutor, even if she were physically able to speak. The two girls' naming her disabilities rather than her subject-position emphasises the gap between their mutual affiliation and her relegation to outsider. Looking back from the narrative present, Twyla 'even now' feels the blush of shame for having used Maggie's disability to other her.

In the scene where they are protesting for and against racial integration, Twyla and Roberta talk, somewhat unexpectedly, about Maggie. Because Roberta thinks Twyla has just called her prejudiced, the issue for them in this argument isn't the treatment of a person with disabilities but the question of whether Maggie was black:

> Maybe I am different now, Twyla. But you're not. You're the same little state kid who kicked a poor old black lady when she was down on the ground. You kicked a black lady and you have the nerve to call me a bigot.

The one-way exchange of name-calling (using something like 'bow-legs' as a term of address rather than reference) is familiar to any stigmatised group but is intensified in racism and sexism. It is always a position that asserts entitlement, thus Roberta claims an one-up position to Twyla when she challenges Twyla's right to call her (Roberta) 'a bigot'. This name-calling and challenge to name-calling queers the categories by calling attention to the one-way exchange as never entirely one-way. It all depends on who is who, who claims to be what, and who does she think she is, anyway?

On all the other occasions when Twyla and Roberta meet as adults, Twyla as narrator conveys their meetings through untagged dialogue, mostly containing chit-chat typical of chance meetings. These dialogues convey the women's growing distance from each other, in which they 'passed like strangers'. Their last encounter presents a strong contrast, when their exchange of dialogue attempts to reconcile their shared but conflicting memories, including their disagreement over 'that business about Maggie'. Importantly, this final meeting, including Roberta's confession and her tearful question about Maggie's fate, is conveyed almost entirely in dialogue. Morrison does not resolve their uncertainty by giving Twyla a narrator's opportunity to sum up the story's meaning, but leaves the significance hanging in the silence that follows Roberta's question about what the hell happened, a silence suffused with their shared sense of shame.

'Recitatif' begins with Twyla's speaking dismissively of Roberta's and her own vulnerability. 'People want to put their arms around you when you tell them you were in a shelter, but it really wasn't bad.' The story ends with Roberta voicing concern about Maggie's vulnerability: 'Oh shit, Twyla. Shit, shit, shit. What the hell happened to Maggie?'. The dismissal, in the first instance, is also a sign to the reader, here rendered as 'people', not to sentimentalise, not to be the kind of people who would 'put their arms around you'. The story's ending similarly repudiates sentimentality, signified in part by the repetition of 'shit' four times. The first 'oh shit', could simply be the frame for a casual comment, a discourse marker for a mistake acknowledged. But the three 'shits' that follow are not casual at all; they forcefully acknowledge a state of distress. From the beginning, Morrison asks us to shift away from sympathy, and at the end, she asks us to recognise shame.[25] Twyla-as-narrator has already claimed shame on her own behalf, as an 'I' ('it shames me even now') rather than as a 'we, white people' or 'we, black people', thus avoiding the reification of entrenched power relationships.[26] Here Roberta embodies shame by shielding herself from her friend's gaze and then dropping that shield: 'Roberta lifted her hands from the table top and covered her face with her palms. When she took them away she really was crying'. Neither woman is shaming the other; neither assumes the one-up position that would affirm either white people's or black people's implicit right to put the racial other down. Morrison undercuts Twyla's earlier epiphany and withholds the feel-good moment that this moment of mutuality might have supplied. Significantly, the two women don't embrace while Roberta's question hangs in the hair, unanswered. The 'insanity of racism' and the misprision of disability won't be solved by sentimental reconciliations bridging the alterity between the African-American and the white, the not-yet-disabled and the disabled. Read through our two feminist narratologies, the narrative and linguistic structures of 'Recitatif' make this as clear as Twyla's, Roberta's and Maggie's identities are obscure.

Notes

1. See Susan S. Lanser, 'Toward a Feminist Narratology', *Style*, 20, no. 3 (1986), pp. 341–63; Robin Lakoff, 'Language and Woman's Place', *Language in Society*, 2, no. 1 (1973), pp. 45–79; and Sally McConnell-Ginet, *Women and Language in Literature and Society* (Santa Barbara, CA: Praeger, 1980).
2. See Susan S. Lanser, 'Burning Dinners: Feminist Subversions of Domesticity', in Jo Radner (ed.), *Feminist Messages: Coding in Women's Folk Culture* (Urbana: University of Illinois Press, 1993), pp. 36–53; and Gabriella Modan and Amy Shuman, 'Narratives of Reputation: Layerings of Social and Spatial Identities', in D. Schiffrin, A. De Fina, and A. Nylund (eds.), *Telling Stories: Language, Narrative, and Social Life* (Washington, DC: Georgetown University Press, 2010), pp. 83–94.
3. Ruth Page, *Literary and Linguistic Approaches to Feminist Narratology* (New York: Palgrave Macmillan, 2006).
4. Toni Morrison, 'Recitatif', in Amiri Baraka and Amina Baraka (eds.), *Confirmation: An Anthology of African-American Women* (New York: Morrow, 1983).
5. Toni Morrison, *Playing in the Dark* (New York: Vintage, 1992), p. xi.
6. See especially Benjamin and Li on the dynamics of race and reading in 'Recitatif'. Shanna Greene Benjamin, 'The Space that Race Creates: An Interstitial Analysis of Toni Morrison's "Recitatif"', *Studies in American Fiction*, 40, no. 1 (2013), pp. 87–106; and Stephanie Li, 'Performing Intimacy Using "Race-Specific, Race-Free Language": Black Private Letters in the Public Sphere', *South Atlantic Quarterly*, 109, no. 2 (2010), pp. 339–56.
7. For discussion of 'the unspeakable', see Judith Roof and Robyn Wiegman, *Who Can Speak?: Authority and Critical Identity* (Urbana: University of Illinois Press, 1995); and Amy Shuman, 'Story Ownership and Entitlement', in Ana De Fina and Alexandra Georgakopoulou-Nunes (eds.), *Handbook of Narrative Analysis* (London: Wiley-Blackwell, 2015), pp. 38–56. For discussion of 'the unnarratable', see Robyn Warhol, 'Neonarrative, or, How to Render the Unnarratable in Realist Fiction and Contemporary Film', in James Phelan and Peter Rabinowitz (eds.), *Blackwell Companion to Narrative Theory* (Oxford: Blackwell, 2005), pp. 220–31. See also Kelly Marsh, *The Submerged Plot and the Mother's Narrative* (Columbus: Ohio State University Press, 2016); and Helen H. Davis, '"I Seemed to Hold Two Lives": Disclosing Circumnarration in *Villette* and *The Picture of Dorian Gray*', *Narrative*, 21, no. 2 (2013), pp. 198–220.
8. Gayatri Chakravorty Spivak, 'Can the Subaltern Speak?', in Cary Nelson and Lawrence Grossberg (eds.), *Marxism and the Interpretation of Culture* (London: Macmillan, 1988), pp. 24–8.
9. William Faulkner, *Absalom, Absalom!* (New York: Random House, 1936).
10. Toni Morrison, 'Interview: The Art of Fiction No. 134', *The Paris Review*, 128 (1993). http://www.theparisreview.org/interviews/1888/the-art-of-fiction-no-134-toni-morrison.
11. For discussion of the subnarratable, see Warhol, 'Neonarrative, or, How to Render the Unnarratable'; Marsh, *The Submerged Plot and the Mother's Narrative*; and Davis, '"I Seemed to Hold Two Lives"'.
12. Rimmon-Kenan defines ambiguity for narratology as the '"conjunction" of exclusive disjuncts, where double and multiple meaning are based on the conjunction of compatible readings, irony on disjunction, allegory on equivalence,

and indeterminacy on the absence of any necessary logical operator'. See Shlomith Rimmon-Kenan, 'Ambiguity and Narrative Levels: Christine Brooke-Rose's Thru', *Poetics Today*, 3, no. 1 (1982), pp. 21–32 (p. 21).
13. Katharine Young, 'Indirection in Storytelling', *Western Folklore*, 37, no. 1 (1978), pp. 46–55 (p. 51). Young differentiates between formal indirection and structural indirection, p. 53.
14. See Susan Ervin-Trip, 'Is Sybil There? The Structure of Some American English Directives', *Language in Society*, 5 (1976), pp. 25–66 (pp. 42–5), for a discussion of how hints work, that is, how implicit information is conveyed and received.
15. William Labov, 'Uncovering the Event Structure of Narrative', *Georgetown University Round Table*, (2003), pp. 63–83.
16. Michael Silverstein, 'Indexical Order and the Dialectics of Sociolinguistic Life', *Language & Communication*, 23, no. 3 (2003), pp. 193–229.
17. Peggy Phelan, *Unmarked: The Politics of Performance* (New York: Routledge, 2003), p. 10.
18. Valentina Pagliai, 'Unmarked Racializing Discourse, Facework, and Identity in Talk about Immigrants in Italy', *Journal of Linguistic Anthropology*, 21, no. 1 (2011), pp. E94–E112 (p. 195), argues, 'The introduction of racializing discourse as unmarked, in conversation, has the effect of restricting the *residential* agency of addressees by restricting their control over the expression of a sign ... by deciding when and where to engage in such discourse'.
19. Mary Bucholtz and Kira Hall, 'Theorizing Identity in Language and Sexuality Research', *Language in Society*, 33, no. 4 (2004), pp. 469–515 (p. 372).
20. Howard Sklar argues that the 'story's ethical center lies in the changes in the way that the two girls/women perceive Maggie'. See '"What the Hell Happened to Maggie?": Stereotype, Sympathy, and Disability in Toni Morrison's "Recitatif"', *Journal of Literary & Cultural Disability Studies*, 5, no. 2 (2011), pp. 137–54 (p. 148).
21. David T. Mitchell and Sharon L. Snyder, *Narrative Prosthesis: Disability and the Dependencies of Discourse* (Ann Arbor: University of Michigan Press, 2000). Although Mitchell and Snyder use the term 'prosthesis' critically, the metaphorical use potentially undermines a central concern among disability studies scholars about the more general use of people with disabilities as metaphors for life's obstacles. See Brenda Jo Brueggemann, 'An Enabling Pedagogy: Meditations on Writing and Disability', *JAC*, (2001), pp. 791–820.
22. Toni Morrison, *The Bluest Eye* (New York: Holt, Rinehard, and Winston, 1970).
23. Of course, more could be said, and more has been said, about disability and the privileged role of speaking and the aestheticisation of silence. For example, see Brueggemann's discussion of what she calls 'the will to speech'. Brenda Jo Brueggemann, 'Delivering Disability, Willing Speech', in Carrie Sandahl and Philip Auslander (eds.), *Bodies in Commotion: Disability and Performance* (Ann Arbor: University of Michigan Press), pp. 17–29.
24. Such repetition brilliantly echoes Jorge Luis Borges' brilliant (repetition intentional) argument in the story of Pierre Menard, who rewrote Cervantes' *Don Quixote* word for word, but the text is entirely different because Menard wrote it much later. See Jorge Borges, 'Pierre Menard, Author of the Quixote'. *Labyrinths: Selected Stories and Other Writings* (New York: New Directions, 1964), pp. 36–44.

25. Elspeth Probyn writes that shame 'dramatically questions taken-for-granted distinctions between affect, emotion, biography, and the places in which we live our daily lives'. See 'Everyday Shame', *Cultural Studies*, 18, no. 2–3 (2004), pp. 328–49 (p. 328).
26. See Elizabeth A. Povinelli, 'The State of Shame: Australian Multiculturalism and the Crisis of Indigenous Citizenship', *Critical Inquiry*, 24, no. 2 (1998), pp. 575–610, on sympathy and shame.

Disclosure statement

No potential conflict of interest was reported by the authors.

Index

Absalom, Absalom! 95
action 17–18, 28–9, 31, 33–4, 36, 63–6, 68–9, 77, 79–80, 84, 86, 96, 98, 102–3
aesthetic figures 28–31
ambiguity 4, 17, 84, 87, 95–8
American television 45, 49–50
archival sensibility 32
assassination 6, 58–9, 61–2, 67, 69–71
assumptions 5, 11, 14, 16–17, 61, 75, 77, 93, 95–6, 100

Beecher, Jonathan 25
belatedness 52
Best Friends Forever (BFF) 5–6, 42–4, 50–1, 54–5
blindness 84–5, 89, 94
body schema 7, 62, 68
Bringing Out Roland Barthes 21
Butler, Judith 65

Caudwell, Sarah 17
class difference 100
classical narratology 2
cognition 6, 59–60, 63–4, 66, 70–1
cognitive narratology 6, 58–60, 63–4
collective voice 18
conceptual persona 28
conceptual personae 28–30
Coykendall, Abby 22
'Cyberage Narratology' 19

disability 8, 91, 95, 99–103, 105–6
Edelman, Marian Wright 76
embodied cognitive narratology 65, 68, 70
embodied edge 69–71
embodied experience 63–70
embodied feminist narratology 71
embodied resonances 63, 69–70

embodiment 7, 60–3, 65, 70; modes of 62–3
entanglements 28
epiphany 91, 95, 102–3, 106

fake 5, 44–5, 47, 50–2, 54–5
Faking It 44, 47
Faulkner, William 95
feedback loop 63, 66, 68, 70
female brains 6, 59–60
female characters 18, 49, 54
female desire 43, 51–2
female friendship 44, 50–2, 55
feminism 2–3, 8, 12, 28, 58, 89, 92
feminist history 7, 28, 30, 38
feminist narratologists 8, 91, 95, 100
feminist narratology 2–7, 11–12, 17, 19–20, 28, 30, 59–60, 78, 92, 106
Ferris, Joshua 18
fictions 3, 17–18, 103
film 13, 46, 49, 78, 85–6, 94
fonds 31–3
Fourier, Charles 26, 34
friendship 5, 43–5, 50–5, 84

Garréta, Anne 17
gay 16, 18, 48–9, 52–3
gaze 78, 83, 85, 103
gender 3–6, 8, 11–13, 15, 17–21, 59–60, 64, 66, 68, 70, 77, 80, 82, 91–2; ambiguity 84, 87; differences 59–60; identity 5, 10; indeterminacies 78–9
gender-ambiguous narrator 17–18
genderqueer voices 17
Goliard, Lisa 82–4, 89

habitus 64
Hamid, Moshin 14
heterodiegesis 13, 78–9
heterodiegetic narration 17, 20

INDEX

heterodiegetic narrators 15–16, 18
homodiegetic narrators 17–18

identity 15, 17, 43, 52, 77, 84, 86–7, 101;
  categories 20, 101
Insignificant Others 14
interpellation 64
invisibility 2, 8, 75, 77, 84

Labov, William 97
Lakoff, Robin 92
language 2, 17, 51, 63, 66–70, 81–3, 86
'Language and Woman's Place' 92
Lanser's rule 19
lesbian desire 42–3, 50–1, 54–5
lesbianism 5, 43–5, 47–51, 54–5
lesbian relationships 44, 50–1
LGBTQ characters 45, 47, 49, 53
linguistic anthropologists 91, 97–8, 101
Literary and Linguistic Approaches to Feminist Narratology 92
literary feminist narratologies 91–2, 95
love triangle 48

Macauley, Stephen 14
Margolis, Eleanor 44
McBean, S. 5
McCallum, E. L. 21
McConnell-Ginet, Sally 92
memories 26, 36, 38, 76, 83–4, 87, 103, 106
middle-class woman 66–7, 70
Miller, D. A. 21, 46
Morrison, Toni 8, 93, 95

narration 15, 18, 20–1, 33, 61, 68, 93, 96, 103
narrative discourse 13, 92, 95
narrative possibilities 15, 44, 48, 50
narrative theory 6, 14, 22, 45–6, 60
Narrative Theory Unbound: Queer and Feminist Interventions 78
narrative voice 3–5, 10–14, 16–17, 20, 78
narratology 2–3, 12, 22, 59, 78, 91–2
narrator's gender 19
Needham, Gary 46
negativity 52–3
The New Statesman 44
novels 19–20, 79, 89

orphanage 93, 100, 102, 104
otherness 94–5, 98

Page, Ruth 92
performance 54, 64–8, 87
power 5, 7–8, 29, 35, 75–80, 83–4, 86, 89
predictions 6, 60, 63–4, 69–71

queer author 5, 16–17, 21
queerer narratology 78
queer identity 43–4, 52–3
queer narratives 5, 42, 45, 54–5
queer narratology 12, 75, 89
queer narrators 5, 14–15, 17
queerness 4–5, 14, 20, 22, 45–8, 51–5, 78
Queer orientation 14
queer rhythm 21
queer temporalities 46, 52, 76
queer temporality theory 46

racial identity 8, 84–5, 89, 93–4, 100, 104
'Recitatif' 8, 91, 93–8, 101, 103, 106
recitative 93–4
The Reluctant Fundamentalist 14
representational visibility 75–6, 89

same-sex 43–4, 51–2, 55
sculpture 29, 88
Sedgwick, Eve Kosofsky 21
shame 53, 103, 105–6
Smith, Zadie 14
social class 66, 100
social identities 17, 77
surveillance 82–3, 87
Susan S. Lanser 10, 46, 78
Swing Time 14

television 45–50, 53
temporalities 5, 18, 45, 49–52
Thatcher, Margaret 6–7, 58–9, 61–3, 67–71
Then We Came to the End 18
theory of mind 59–60

unnarratable, experiments 95

Véret-Gay, Désirée 7, 25, 32
Villarejo, Amy 46
visibility 5, 7, 54, 75–9, 86–7, 101

Winterson, Jeanette 12
Women and Language in Literature and Society 92
women workers 36
Written on the Body 12

9780367681128